WHAT I SAW

SAW

AT THE SECOND COMING

WHAT I SAW

AT THE SECOND COMING

THE BIG STORY
PART I

BY R.J. MORTON

TABLE OF CONTENTS

PROLOGUE

He who speaks does not know.
He who knows does not speak.
— Lao Zi

———◆———

"But concerning that day and hour no one knows,
not even the angels of heaven, nor the Son, but the Father
only."
— Matthew 24:36

The world had no idea the "First Coming" had happened until long after the brief life and revolution of Jesus Christ.

The accounts of ordinary people who shared life experiences with the son of God are largely unrecorded. The ripple from his life's impact went all but unnoticed in the sea of humanity during his time on Earth.

Likewise, the "Second Coming" which has already happened according to adherents to Sun Myung Moon's teachings was a mere blip or three in the news. If he was "the one," he came indeed as a "thief in the night." [Revelations 16:15]

But his worldwide ministry in the last four decades of the twentieth century took place in the "information age" with explosive advances in modern communications technology.

What happened?

Why the effective silence of his followers said to believe they represent a new lineage; That their bloodlines had been engrafted to the "Tree of Life" as the lineal descendants of "True Parents"; That such is the goal of God's providential messianic dispensation?[1]

---

1   According to the "Divine Principle" explanation of the Holy Bible

Surely this would be news to shout from the rooftops. Did they lack the courage of their convictions? Did their words fall on deaf ears? Did Sun Myung Moon get a fair trial in the worldwide court of public opinion?

What follows is a record of one eyewitness to the birth, growth and internal debates and wars in the media foundation established by Sun Myung Moon that within years of his death had fallen largely silent.

That foundation could have established the cognitive landscape for a worldwide audience to receive his message, still largely unreported.

Such is conceivably a far greater and deeper truth than the mere chronicling of current events by newspapers and digital-electronic media.

So, this is not the story that some believe will transform the world. That story has already been written by Sun Myung Moon himself, including his "Divine Principle" [https://christkingdomgospel.org/archives/divine-principle/] and his spoken words in "Cheon Seong Gyeong" [http://www.unification.net/csg/CheonSeongGyeong.pdf]

———————◆———————

"So Christ, having been offered once to bear the sins of many, will appear a second time, not to deal with sin but to save those who are eagerly waiting for him."
— Hebrews 9:28

———————◆———————

The 'Second Coming' of Christ, often associated with the apocalyptic "end times" is no laughing matter. Or is it?

Based on my own rare "mystical" experiences (noted briefly in Chapter 2), I would suggest that the God of Abraham, Isaac and Jacob has a finely tuned sense of humor. Dullards and ideologues are often humorless unlike more spirited and inquisitive lovers of freedom. Surely the Creator of the Universe does not have taciturnity as His defining characteristic. Sun Myung Moon himself was often in high spirits when he spoke extemporaneously. But it was sometimes as if he were trying to cheer up not only his followers but also God Himself. After all, as Sun Myung Moon exclusively taught, the Creator as a Parent had suffered far more heartbreak than any of His children.

The monumental struggles between Good and Evil, as recorded in the Holy Bible from the beginning of history to the First Coming of Christ, and then through the bitter and bloody wars of the twentieth century have not ended. But Sun Myung Moon said his "Divine Principle", the Cheon Seong Gyeong and selected speeches were the "Completed Testament", connecting the dots of the "Old" and "New" Testaments" of the Bible.

He often expressed frustration that those closest to him did not grasp the significance of his "Words of Life"[2] from God and the "True Love" he freely gave and lived. That testament culminating in the eternal marriage "blessing" of

---

2 Prayer before sermon on Sept. 6, 1959: "Please do not reject us. Embrace us. You know that we are lonely because we do not have a place to rest our hearts and minds. Please comfort us during this hour. Please appear before us with this heart and guide us as our subject partner of eternal life. Give us words of life which can penetrate our minds and bodies." https://www.unification.net/1959/590906.html

the innumerable couples who were transformed by them were what mattered most, he said, not the many organizations he set up only to frequently change or erase them. Among such organizations that no longer exist was the Unification Church.

We are left to wonder how that "Kingdom of God on Earth" would have looked had Sun Myung Moon been welcomed and attended in the "Fatherland", his native Korea.

His spoken and written record[3] reveals how he prepared for that Kingdom and what Jesus envisioned at the First Coming. He taught that the Kingdom would not come in an ethereal flash of light but as a concrete concept that required a nation. Israel had been prepared as the chosen nation to receive the Messiah but had not recognized him. Likewise, he said, Korea had been prepared as the chosen nation to receive the Lord of the Second Advent.

"For as the lightning comes from the east and shines as far as the west,
so will be the coming of the Son of Man."
— Matthew 24:27

---

3   That record explains the origin of evil in the world and the ideal God had for his children in the beginning. It unmasks the ultra-secretive Satan, the evil angel who stole the first family from God and thus owns humanity as the original ancestor of all. It reveals God's principles of creation and restoration, the literal "keys" to regenerate God's family of man.

Anti-communist Sun Myung Moon, left, and communist Kim Il-Sung met in Pyongyang, North Korea in December 1991. Both supported a unified Korea, the "Fatherland". / Video image.

Sun Myung Moon, known by his followers as "True Father" established many international organizations and media, including The Washington Times and the Korean Segye Ilbo. But his goal was the "Kingdom of God on Earth."

Whereas Christianity focused on individual salvation in the realm after death, he taught that the fulfillment of Christianity was foreshadowed by the Lord's Prayer: "Thy Kingdom come, thy will be done, on Earth as it is in Heaven."[4] Thus, he conducted mass weddings worldwide as the basis for family-level salvation to eventually establish the lineage of God on Earth. Known as the "Blessing," this wedding is

---

4   Matthew 6:9-13

the sacrament for his followers who believe their union is eternal and not "until death do us part". Moreover, it is the basis for salvation on earth as well as in heaven. "Blessed families" are considered the building blocks for the Kingdom of God. Again, as Jesus prayed in the Lord's Prayer: "Thy Kingdom come, they will be done on Earth as it is in Heaven."

He taught hundreds of thousands of Koreans his ideology of unification based on "Godism" as a critical alternative to communism. Such, he said, was a prerequisite and practical necessity for unification with the Marxist Leninist North.

North Korea operates from its presumed ideological purity relative to the former USSR and Communist China. Significantly the Pyongyang regime also insists that it alone represents the true Korean cultural soul. Post-war South Korea, that became a booming Asian Tiger under President Park Chung-Hee and his Stanford-educated economists, has always been dismissed by the Communist North as a corrupt capitalist "puppet" of the American "imperialists". Despite the benefits of wealth and prestige, many South Koreans in their heart of hearts have had no answer for this claim from the North where the leader has been treated as the fatherly king, a deeply-rooted theme of Korean history and innumerable and always popular classical Korean films.

Of all South Koreans, only Sun Myung Moon claimed an ideology superior to North Korea's. What's more, he directly and publicly proclaimed that doctrine during a homecoming visit to North Korea in 1991 at the risk of his life, setting the stage for a historic meeting with his life-long enemy. Remarkably he embraced and bonded with the dictator Kim

Il-Sung in whose death camp he had nearly died during and just after the Incheon Landing in September 1950 by U.S. and UN forces led by Gen. Douglas MacArthur in early stages of the Korean War.

Only months before his historic trip to Pyongyang in late 1991, he had sponsored a World Media Conference in Moscow where he met with Mikhail Gorbachev and urged him to embrace freedom of religion and to open diplomatic relations with South Korea. Gorbachev agreed to and followed through on those conditions both of which would have been unthinkable for his predecessors. Only a hostile and dismissive global establishment and media prevented Sun Myung Moon from being acknowledged for such monumental national and international accomplishments.

Indeed, his youngest son and designated successor Hyung Jin Moon takes very seriously indeed the coming "Kingdom of God on Earth". He and his older brother Kook Jin Moon, founder of Kahr Arms, have charged that the official leadership of the movement his father founded has selectively rewritten and erased his words and de-emphasized his very significance.

In 2015, they and their "Sanctuary Church"[5] announced that their mother, Hak-Ja Han, had conducted what amounted to the theft of her husband's assets, legacy and worldwide foundation. Later, she proclaimed herself the "Only Begotten Daughter of God" and reportedly suggested that her husband, unlike her, had original sin.

Also in 2015, on Oct. 15, Hyung Jin Moon announced

---

5   World Peace and Unification Sanctuary (WPUS) commonly known as Sanctuary Church

the "Constitution of the United States of Cheon Il Guk", the Kingdom of God on Earth[6].

The first paragraph of its Preamble is clear as to the Providential intent and reads as follows:

> Cheon Il Guk, The Kingdom of God (and/or Heaven), a sovereign and actual nation does not yet exist in this world but is the long-awaited culmination of the End of Time as prophesied in the Biblical Scripture. The Divine Principle and the Eight Great Textbook Curriculum revealed by True Father, Christ at His second Coming, is the spiritual foundation of this Constitution. It is upon this foundation of these eternal truths that the future nation of Cheon Il Guk will be politically and legally established. This Constitution is not an ecclesiastical Constitution of a church or religious body, but is a constitution for a real and sovereign, future nation, being the literal fruit of God's Providence. All history longs and awaits this future Kingdom of God.

Many of Sun Myung Moon's aging early followers try to transcend the profound divisions in their faith community following his death and now take those life-changing teachings and "The Divine Principle" for granted. What was a revelation and a born-again experience in youth has been assimilated, diluted and often relegated to a footnote as earthly life winds down. Lives once transformed by the "Principle" are now primarily defined by the real time screenplay of daily events immersed in the temporal and evolving virtual reality and popular culture on Earth.

---

6   https://www.sanctuary-pa.org/constitution#constitution

WHAT I SAW AT THE SECOND COMING...

But those "Words of Life" still exist and are said to be the "New Truth" foretold in the Bible (John 8:32). Before the life and times of Sun Myung Moon, they were nowhere to be found.

Readers could check it out for themselves and should take no one else's word for it.

Certainly, they should be prepared to dismiss as journalistic malpractice much of the published reporting about the man and his teachings. The "media" which so many trusted to faithfully record the "first draft of history" has been absent or simply wrong about many important stories related to the struggles for freedom against sinister and Godless ideologies in the 20th and 21st centuries. Likewise, the "media" arguably missed this, the biggest story of all time.

The actual words of Sun Myung Moon are online and widely published. As Jesus said, "he who has ears to hear, let him hear."

———————◆———————

"For as were the days of Noah, so will be the coming of the Son of Man. For as in those days before the flood they were eating and drinking,
marrying and giving in marriage, until the day when Noah entered the ark, and they were unaware until the flood came and swept them all away, so will be the coming of the Son of Man."
— Matthew 24:37-39

———————◆———————

The following account will not attempt to proselytize or persuade in matters of faith and Divine intervention. Such for each individual is the most personal, precious and essential knowledge.

No, what follows is merely a record of what I, a journalist, saw at the "Second Coming."

Because Lao Zi had it right. The ultimate truth belongs exclusively to each individual.

CHAPTER 1

MESSIAH AS INVESTIGATIVE JOURNALIST

Since we are at the time of the Completed Testament Age ...
it is time for your families to settle following my words.
Therefore, when you listen to my words, you should not treat
them casually. I risked my life, urgently teaching you what I
have to say and desiring to leave behind at least these words.
You must understand this.
— Sun Myung Moon (292-122, 1998.3.28)

The Messiah is generally viewed as an other-worldly or apocalyptic figure who will purge the world of wickedness and set things right, immediately if not sooner.

Sun Myung Moon's teaching about the Messiah was more down to Earth. The restored Adam would come as a man born naturally like all other men who have ever lived and died, he said. And no, he would not be a dictator.

Sun Myung Moon (1920-2012) was a spiritual teacher, businessman, and philanthropist whose followers consider him the "Lord of the Second Advent", the Messiah. And they believe he bequeathed his divine essence through his bloodline and the "Blessing" of eternal marriage to all who

Sun Myung Moon as a student at Waseda University in Japan in 1941. / Public Domain

would receive it, from generation to generation.

His "Divine Principle" connects the dots in the Bible and states that both the Creation and the evolution of civilization after "The Fall" happened over time periods in accordance with the "Principle of Growth" and "Historical Parallels."

Thus the "Second Coming" of Christ would once again test the Free Will of all men and women as at all other critical providential junctures including the Fall[1] in the Biblical Garden of Eden, the great Flood and the First Coming. It would not be imposed by violent and apocalyptic Divine intervention.

The remarkable success of this North Korea-born anti-communist thought leader in attracting young followers in the East and the West in the 1970s provided an irresistible story line to journalists. The secular mass media in the West exploited prejudices deemed acceptable towards Orientals and conservative anti-communists to project a threatening image of Sun Myung Moon as the ultimate evil incarnate, more menacing and sinister than the worst Nazi or Fascist.

Persecution from leading organized religions made him even more universally controversial. Christians and Jews of all stripes saw him take their youth as followers and concluded after a cursory review provided by press accounts, that he was a heretic, a Pied Piper or, worse, the Anti-Christ[2].

A public relations study commissioned by the Unification Church in the early 1990s[3] at the suggestion of myself and

---

1 "Had Adam and Eve consulted with God, there would have been no Fall. They should have asked the question, "The Archangel is doing such and such, so what shall we do?" Then God could have responded to them. The act of asking was their portion of responsibility. They were free to ask. However, they established a horizontal relationship without asking God. That was the problem. Because they acted without asking, a problem occurred." (Cheon Seong Gyeong, by Sun Myung Moon, 33-241, 1970.8.16)

2 I John 2:18: Little children, it is the last time. And as ye have heard that Antichrist shall come, even now are there many antichrists, whereby we know that this is the last time.

3 Study by the Huckabee and Rodgriguez research firm in Sacramento, California.

other sympathetic and media-savvy types found that even then, as the persecution of his church was waning, Sun Myung Moon's negative ratings equaled or surpassed those of Adolph Hitler.

But this was no Jim Jones or Joseph Stalin. Mass suicides and genocide were not what this "cult" was all about. Young hippies were transformed through born-again experiences into clean-shaven, well-groomed citizens.

What then was so sinister about Sun Myung Moon?

His real threat, like that of Donald J. Trump in 2015 who emerged on the world stage three years after Sun Myung Moon left it, was to the established order.

Like Jesus Christ, he was a God-loving revolutionary who challenged the moral authority and credibility of an increasingly corrupt political-cultural ruling class.

Merely being a Christian conservative would make him controversial in the post-World War II West, but what was he teaching? What was it about his "New Truth" that posed such a threat?

Shoe-leather Journalism of the Cosmic Kind

Sun Myung Moon appeared on the scene in the United States and Europe in the 1970s following the work of an advance team of missionaries and early members teaching his "Divine Principle." Two-day workshops featured a series of lectures with chalk-board diagrams that included comprehensive Biblical and historical detail.

The lectures addressed the same topics: Ideal of Creation, the Human Fall, the Meaning of the "Last Days", the Mission of Jesus, the Meaning of Resurrection, and Post-Biblical history concluding with the Second Coming of the Messiah. They also enlarged upon Jesus' teaching that God is love.[4]

To truly know Him is to encounter a God of unbearable suffering[5], Sun Myung Moon exclusively taught. If God was indeed "Heavenly Father", how could he not be heartbroken at the suffering of His children in this Hell on Earth, he asked.

The Divine Principle was not delivered by God on tablets of stone, as Moses received the Ten Commandments. Rather, the "Completed Testament", was written after agonizing research by Sun Myung Moon that began on April 17, 1935, when at the age of 15 he says he met Jesus in prayer near his birthplace in North Korea.[6] He completed the first draft of the Divine Principle in Busan, South Korea some 15 years later.

That research involved detailed study of the Bible (simultaneously in three languages[7]) and all-night prayers which included encounters with primary sources in the spirit world.

---

4   1 John 4:7-11: 7 Beloved, let us love one another: for love is of God; and every one that loveth is born of God, and knoweth God. 8 He that loveth not knoweth not God; for God is love. 9 In this was manifested the love of God toward us, because that God sent his only begotten Son into the world, that we might live through him. 10 Herein is love, not that we loved God, but that he loved us, and sent his Son to be the propitiation for our sins. 11 Beloved, if God so loved us, we ought also to love one another.

5   Interview with Dr. Frederick Sontag, http://www.reverendsunmyungmoon.org/life_interview.html: Throughout history no one has suffered more than God. He has suffered because his own children fell away from him. Ever since the Fall, God has been working tirelessly for the restoration of mankind. People do not know this brokenhearted aspect of God. .... From their own experience of suffering and tragedy, Koreans can readily understand God's sorrow and broken heart.

6   Breen, Michael, "Sun Myung Moon, The Early Years, 1920-53.". Refuge Books, 1997, pp. 31-32.

7   In his autobiography, 'As a Peace-Loving Global Citizen' [The Washington Times Foundation, 2009], Sun Myung Moon wrote that while a student in Japan he had three Bibles always opened on his desk, one in English, one in Korean and one in Japanese all with notes in tiny script written in the margins.

He did not believe what he was told during those experiences and checked them out.[8] One might say that the process entailed shoe leather journalism of the cosmic kind. It continued even when he was imprisoned in South Korea and Japan where he practiced what he preached based in part on what he was processing and validating.

The cruelest early persecution of Sun Myung Moon occurred after he acted on inspiration and left his young family in the South to preach the gospel in the newly communist North Korea where he had been born. Imprisoned in a labor-death camp at Hungnam, he was liberated only following the Incheon landing by U.S. forces under Gen. Douglas MacArthur's command and the push northward early in the Korean War.

A riveting, day-by-day account of the sometimes-hair-raising experiences and spiritual phenomena of those early days was researched and written by journalist Michael Breen based on dozens of in-depth personal interviews of those who came into contact with Sun Myung Moon. He excluded official Unification Church accounts.[9]

Why couldn't the process of discovering his New Truth have been easier, with this spiritual leader merely receiving the Word by automatic writing? He said he had no choice but to personally restore or "indemnify" the failures of human responsibility since the beginning of time and continuing to the present era.

An objective assessment of the lives of Jesus Christ and

---

8 Breen, Ibid.
9 Breen, Michael, "Sun Myung Moon, The Early Years, 1920-53,". Refuge Books, 1997, 191 pages.

Sun Myung Moon would indeed show that being the alleged Messiah is no walk in the park.

Championing American Press Freedom

My meetings with him, few and brief though they were, reinforced a conclusion reached by serving as a "participant-observer"[10] in his media companies from 1976 to early 2013: Sun Myung Moon understood the media challenge in the United States in ways his disciples whom he charged with running those newspapers struggled to grasp. It certainly went far beyond an exercise in large-scale public relations for a new religion. What he envisioned was much more profound. After all it was the post-World War II mass media that had redefined reality for billions of people worldwide in ways that excluded God and the essence of Judeo-Christianity. Some might say that this doctrine stemmed from an evil, Orwellian force seeking to negate the very causal factors in the rise of advanced western civilization and instead consolidate the foundations of "Hell on Earth."

My frank and direct exchanges with him on the realities of daily American newspapers also persuaded me that he grasped the unique mindset of working journalists in a way that few outside that profession do.

He extended his unwavering support for my tenure and that of other editors and reporters at his media properties who might otherwise have been disposed of by managers convinced they knew best.

---

10 See Chapter 3, "Method and Approach: Participant Observer as Pediatric Historian," of the author's master's degree thesis at the University of Texas at Austin (1977, Robert J Morton) and book: The News World of New York City: A Retrospective, 2023, Origin 2021 Publishing).

Certainly, all top editors at The Washington Times said they had never experienced the degree of editorial independence without interference from the ownership that they enjoyed at The Times. That was my experience as well. Furthermore, the "bright white line" between the business and editorial divisions was rigorously enforced. Naturally all publications were expected to wage war on Godless ideological and cultural forces.

As this is written in 2022, few people know the name of the man who launched newspapers in New York, Washington, DC, Tokyo, Seoul, the Middle East and Latin America[11].

Sun Myung Moon's telegraphed his dedication to the concept of Freedom of the Press in empowering free peoples to guide their own governments by creating in 1978 the Free Press International news service (his initiative, I was told). He went on to establish multiple newspapers at an enormous outlay, especially The Washington Times. All of those newspaper had editorial freedom and were free of commercial, political or religious interference. Unlike, for example, the Christian Science Monitor, any allied organization that had a position it wished to advocate in those publications had to take out a full-page paid advertisement.

The enormous investment he made in his media properties, which never achieved profitability despite his continuous demand that they do so, was (I have concluded) an expression of his love for the nations they served. His other mul-

---

11 New York News World, New York City Tribune, The Washington Times, Sekai Nippo, Segye Ilbo, Middle East Times, Ultimas Noticias, Tiempos del Mundo.

Sun Myung Moon signs the first editions of The Washington Times in 1982. / Robert Morton

tiple businesses that did not succeed were closed and much of the profits from those that did went to the media properties, most notably The Washington Times. That outpouring of love was answered by the ridicule of the established media which dismissed serious attention to the man and his message. Such institutional rejection also influenced the senior leadership of The Washington Times which used legal counsel to remind him that his money was welcome, but his direct input was not. Keeping Sun Myung Moon at a distance failed, however, to shield the paper and its employees from the scorn of the political media establishment.

If indeed Sun Myung Moon is the second coming of Christ, one might surmise that the American media reaped what they sowed in disparaging and dismissing him. The legacy media would later lose not only profitability but also credibility with at least the conservative half of the American public. Indeed, the corruption of major cultural and media institutions and the loss of their integrity became crystal clear for all to see during and following the miraculous 2016 campaign and election of President Donald J Trump.[12]

The Free Press Foundation, which I independently established in late 2016 and which has no affiliation or financial connection with any other organization, seeks to restore those lost standards.

> The Free Press was cherished by America's Founding Fathers and serves the public good by holding the powerful accountable to individual citizens: Ours is a government "of the people, by the people and for the people." — *https://freepressfoundation.org/why-we-exist/*

Journalists as 'Misfits'

Once upon a time (in the 1970s when I entered the Journalism graduate program at the University of Texas) mass communications and media studies were desired college majors in the United States and "journalist" was a respected profession. That was not always true and is certainly no longer the case (in 2022) as most polls find that journalists' credibility with the public is just as bad, and often worse, than that of members of Congress.

The late Washington Times Editor Wesley Pruden included the following characterization from an Arkansas town of his youth in his remarks to visiting groups to the newspaper [roughly paraphrased]:

> One prominent couple described their children as follows: "Our oldest son is our pride and joy. He is a min-

---

12 It should be noted that the emergence of Trump on the national political landscape occurred in 2015, the same year that Sun Myung Moon's designated heir and successor Hyung Jin Moon "broke his silence" and established his "Sanctuary Church" after having been removed as the top leader of the worldwide Unification Movement by his mother, Hak Ja Han.

ister of the Gospel. Our second son did very well in school and is a doctor. Our youngest son never amounted to much. We sent him downtown to edit the newspaper."

A longtime editor on the business desk at The Washington Times, the late Dean Honeycutt, had a one-word description of himself and a number of other members of our profession: "Misfits". Some media stars transition to better-paying gigs as PR mavens, press spokespersons, communications specialists at think tanks or elsewhere. Others are hopeless cases: Journalists for life.

Wesley Pruden, who died in July 2019 at 83, is one such example. The famously reclusive Matt Drudge is another. So is the late, great radio talk show host Rush Limbaugh ("talent on loan from God"). All were brilliant at what they did and otherwise would be, if not outcasts, utterly undistinguished in society.

Pruden and I, along with hundreds of other news professionals owed much of our careers and our livelihoods to this Korean man who founded The Washington Times and many other newspapers.

I would argue that Sun Myung Moon's impact on conservative journalism in the United States was enormous. The Washington Times, for example, delivered a powerful and relentless daily drumbeat of news in contrast to that of conservative commentary magazines such as National Review. It launched the careers of many well-known editors, reporters, news executives and pundits during the age of President Ronald Reagan and beyond.

The Washington Times brand, extended by the National

Weekly Edition (which I proposed, created and edited from 1994 to 2013), made its mark on the national media landscape in the 1980s and early 1990s before the dominance of cable news and the Internet. Its business success, a rarity in conservative media, was also due to the direct mail marketing initiatives and diligence of Business Manager Jim Howell.

The late, great Wall Street Journal Editor Robert Bartley credited the National Weekly Edition for covering and reporting from Washington, D.C. the "news that the mainstream media missed or buried."[13]

The Words of Sun Myung Moon

Many consider President Donald Trump the "great disrupter." Before Donald Trump there was Sun Myung Moon. I never felt comfortable calling him "Rev. Moon". Words have meanings. He was no ordinary preacher.

Anyone wanting to know about him could turn to Google and from there to Wikipedia:

Sun Myung Moon (Korean 문선명 Mun Seon-myeong; born Mun Yong-myeong; 25 February 1920 – 3 September 2012) was a Korean religious leader, also known for

---

13 Robert Bartley, the late editor of the Wall Street Journal, wrote in an article for Commentary Magazine about the state of conservative media in February 1997:As the conservative cause prospers, its proliferating publications inevitably have to practice what the business world calls brand differentiation. National Review stakes its ground on outlawing immigration and legalizing drugs. The Weekly Standard becomes the inside-the-Beltway bible. The American Spectator presses Whitewater harder than even I would. My own taste runs to the National Weekly Edition of The Washington Times, a newspaper where you find the news the mainstream media missed or buried. When I thanked him for this tribute, he responded in a personal note of March 4, 1997: "Glad to give you a plug; I meant every word about the Weekly Edition, which ought to be more widely read."

his business ventures and support for political causes. A messiah claimant, he was the founder of the Unification movement (members of which considered him and his wife Hak Ja Han to be their "True Parents"), and of its widely noted "Blessing" or mass wedding ceremony, and the author of its unique theology the Divine Principle. He was an opponent of communism and an advocate for Korean reunification, for which he was recognized by the governments of both North and South Korea. Businesses he promoted included News World Communications, an international news media corporation known for its American subsidiary The Washington Times, and Tongil Group, a South Korean business group (chaebol), as well as various related organizations.

Moon was born in what is now North Korea. When he was a child, his family converted to Christianity. In 1947 he was convicted by the North Korean government of spying for South Korea and given a five-year sentence to the Hŭngnam labor camp. In 1954, he founded the Holy Spirit Association for the Unification of World Christianity in Seoul, South Korea based on conservative, family-oriented teachings from new interpretations of the Bible. In 1971, he moved to the United States and became well known after giving a series of public speeches on his beliefs. In the 1982 case United States v. Sun Myung Moon he was found guilty of willfully filing false federal income tax returns and sentenced to 18 months in federal prison. His case generated protests from clergy and civil libertarians, who said that the trial was biased against him.

Moon was criticized for making high demands of his followers. His wedding ceremonies also drew criticism, especially after they involved members of other churches, including Roman Catholic archbishop Emmanuel Milingo. He was also criticized for his relationships with political and religious figures, including U.S. Presidents Richard Nixon, George H. W. Bush and George W. Bush, Soviet President Mikhail Gorbachev, North Korean President Kim Il Sung.

Like the first messiah, Jesus Christ of Nazareth, Sun Myung had much to say. Limited selections of the words of Jesus are recorded in the Gospels of The Holy Bible in the books of Matthew, Mark, Luke and John. The words of Sun Myung Moon are recorded in his Divine Principle and the Cheon Seong Gyeong[14], a compilation personally approved by him of excerpts from hundreds of public speeches he gave. It is much more readable and accessible than his core teaching, Divine Principle, which requires lectures and seminars to be properly unpacked.

At this point, it is worth emphasizing that their contemporaries did not pay much attention to the words of either alleged Messiah when they were walking the Earth. The words of Jesus, as recorded, gained importance as "Words of Life" and of ultimate Truth long after his lifetime. Those words and the insights they provided proved far more transformative and consequential on a global scale than those of his contemporaries. Will the words of the "returning Lord"

---

14 https://drive.google.com/file/d/1VGgHxuBAZRH4bQdo-mRlAiZbgtYBgZT0/view or
http://www.unification.net/csg/CheonSeongGyeong.pdf

likewise overshadow the "bombshell" exclusives and "narratives" propagated by the chroniclers of the unfolding daily history of our societies?

What made Sun Myung Moon compelling to his followers in the 20th and 21st centuries were both his teachings and (in my estimation) his remarkable mind-body unity with those words. Sun Myung Moon addressed many of the universal questions of human existence including but not limited to:

- Who is God?
- What is the purpose of human life?
- How did Evil originate?
- Who is Satan?
- How could a loving and good God allow Evil to enter and dominate the world occupied by His beloved children?
- What is the meaning of Biblical history that culminated in the life and death of Jesus Christ?
- What is the meaning and significance of history in the post-Biblical era during which many await the coming of the Messiah or, for Christians, the Second Coming of Christ?
- What are the parallels between Biblical and post-Biblical history?
- How would people recognize the Messiah? In what manner would he come to Earth?

Sun Myung Moon's answers to the above questions were not mystical but rational, based on deductions and explanations of the Bible's narrative and symbolism. Are they words of truth? That, as he taught, is for each individual to decide. He practiced what he preached, upholding actions taken by the Free Will of others. He even ordered his disciples not to interfere with personal decisions made by his own children, several of whom reportedly violated his sacrosanct Divine Principle which not only reinforced the Ten Commandments and the Great Commandments taught by Jesus Christ[15] but also detailed the nature and origin of the Original Sin.

The secular media characteristically ignored the spiritual and religious aspects of the man and focused on his business dealings. The "pack journalism" narrative included sinister characterizations of the remarkable influence he held over the lives of his followers deemed devoid of autonomy and "brainwashed". The most shocking aspect of that lifestyle, in a free sex-obsessed popular culture, was their willingness to being matched as couples (yes, "male and female created He them"[16]) and "blessed" by the Messiah in holy marriages regarded by each couple as an eternal sacrament.

Such media accounts discouraged any serious attention to his words or the essence of what he taught. Who then has heard and assimilated his words? Were they the New Truth?

As Jesus often said, "He who has ears to hear, let him hear."

What about the true believers? For all the thousands of hours his followers listened to him speak, how much did they understand and retain as the years passed?

---

15 Matthew 22:36-40
16 Genesis 5:2

Greatest Story of All Time?

It is a testimony to the power of the mass media that during the time Sun Myung Moon walked the Earth, its secular, consensus-based definition of reality ultimately prevailed over that taught by Sun Myung Moon in the minds and lives of even his followers and most of his family members including his wife Hak Ja Han.

Whereas he challenged conventional wisdom in politics and culture at every opportunity with pronouncements based on his own and Biblical teaching, they do not.

The exception is his youngest son, Hyung Jin Moon, whom he anointed in his final years as his successor. "Pastor Sean" as he is known, has publicly and continuously denounced the established U.S. political-cultural order that has come under the atheistic influences of Marxist and "Woke" ideologies. He has sponsored annual "Freedom Festivals" in Pennsylvania and championed the founding principles of the United States of America which have been erased by "progressive" activism. He has also publicly rebuked his mother for seeking to displace her husband as Messiah and for rewriting and deleting many passages of his teachings which Sun Myung Moon had repeatedly directed should never be changed.

Sun Myung Moon's marginalization is not limited to his family and former followers. Prominent conservatives have shied away from the Founder of The Washington Times and while privately loving The Times, have avoided publicly endorsing its value or crediting the controversial man who established it.

Had conventional wisdom been right about Jesus at the time of his cosmically cruel and miserable death, he would be long forgotten, "a poor unfortunate" as one good friend and Jewish scholar described him to me. But conventional wisdom was wrong.

"Be of could cheer, for I have overcome the world," Jesus foretold in his heartrending words of farewell to his disciples[17]. His teaching and example shaped Western civiliza-

---

17 John 16 21st Century King James Version (KJ21)

1 "These things have I spoken unto you, that ye should not lose faith.

2 They shall put you out of the synagogues; yea, the time cometh that whosoever killeth you will think that he doeth God service.

3 And these things will they do unto you, because they have not known the Father, nor Me.

4 But these things have I told you, that when the time shall come, ye may remember that I told you of them. "And these things I said not unto you at the beginning, because I was with you.

5 But now I go My way to Him that sent Me, and none of you asketh Me, 'Whither goest Thou?'

6 But because I have said these things unto you, sorrow hath filled your heart.

7 Nevertheless I tell you the truth. It is expedient for you that I go away, for if I go not away, the Comforter will not come unto you; but if I depart, I will send Him unto you.

8 And when He is come, He will reprove the world concerning sin, and concerning righteousness, and concerning judgment:

9 concerning sin, because they believe not in Me;

10 concerning righteousness, because I go to My Father and ye see Me no more;

11 concerning judgment, because the prince of this world is judged.

12 "I have yet many things to say unto you, but ye cannot bear them now.

13 However when He, the Spirit of Truth, is come, He will guide you into all truth; for He shall not speak from Himself, but whatsoever He shall hear, that shall He speak; and He will show you things to come.

14 He shall glorify Me, for He shall receive of Mine, and shall show it unto you.

15 All things that the Father hath are Mine; therefore I said that He shall take of Mine, and shall show it unto you.

16 A little while, and ye shall not see Me; and again a little while, and ye shall see Me, because I go to the Father."

17 Then said some of His disciples among themselves, "What is this that He saith unto us, 'A little while, and ye shall not see Me; and again a little while, and ye shall see Me,' and, 'because I go to the Father'?"

18 They said therefore, "What is this that He saith, 'A little while'? We cannot tell what He

tion culminating in a Christian nation that emerged as a light unto all nations.

Some would say the United States and major thought leaders with God's guiding hand defeated evil in the great world wars and shattered the communist cancer that threatened to cover the earth. It was during that apocalyptic era that Sun Myung Moon was searching for and proclaiming truth and launching his media empire including The Washington Times. Later in that decade he publicly proclaimed

saith."

19 Now Jesus knew that they were desirous of asking Him, and said unto them, "Do ye inquire among yourselves of what I said, 'A little while, and ye shall not see Me; and again a little while, and ye shall see Me'?

20 Verily, verily I say unto you that ye shall weep and lament, but the world shall rejoice; and ye shall be sorrowful, but your sorrow shall be turned into joy.

21 A woman when she is in travail hath sorrow, because her hour is come; but as soon as she is delivered of the child, she remembereth no more the anguish, for the joy that a man is born into the world.

22 And ye now therefore have sorrow; but I will see you again, and your heart shall rejoice, and your joy no man taketh from you.

23 And in that day ye shall ask Me nothing. Verily, verily I say unto you, whatsoever ye shall ask the Father in My name, He will give it to you.

24 Hitherto have ye asked nothing in My name. Ask and ye shall receive, that your joy may be full.

25 "These things have I spoken unto you in proverbs; but the time cometh when I shall no more speak unto you in proverbs, but I shall show you plainly of the Father.

26 In that day ye shall ask in My name, and I say not unto you that I will pray the Father for you;

27 for the Father Himself loveth you, because ye have loved Me and have believed that I came out from God.

28 I came forth from the Father, and am come into the world. Again, I leave the world and go to the Father."

29 His disciples said unto Him, "Lo, now speakest Thou plainly and speakest no proverb.

30 Now are we sure that Thou knowest all things and needest not that any man should ask Thee. By this we believe that Thou camest forth from God."

31 Jesus answered them, "Do ye now believe?

32 Behold, the hour cometh, yea, is now come, that ye shall be scattered, every man to his own, and shall leave Me alone. And yet I am not alone, because the Father is with Me.

33 These things I have spoken unto you, that in Me ye might have peace. In the world ye shall have tribulation, but be of good cheer: I have overcome the world."

the death of communism, a prophecy that caused consternation to some scholars and analysts who had aligned with him.

The monumental and apocalyptic 1900s and early 2000s, viewed cosmically, were among the ramifications of the sacrifice two thousand years earlier of God's son whose resurrection set the stage for the rise of a new civilization that spanned the globe, he taught.

The great world wars and the re-establishment of the state of Israel was followed by the chronicling of the "End of History" by a Korean man who claims authorship of the greatest story ever written.

CHAPTER 2

AUSTIN, TEXAS AND THE LIGHT

1971

Sometimes, a man has to be totally alone to get his bearings.

Stepping onto the tarmac in the blindingly, white-hot Austin afternoon, I saw no familiar faces waiting and had no numbers to call.

It was August 1971, and I was in Texas, 1135 miles from home, nearest friends and family.

My first passenger jet flight had been awesome, and Texas quickly impressed as upbeat, less humid and more wide-awake than life in the lovely rolling hills of East Tennessee. The University of Texas was super-sized like the iced tea at every restaurant and seemingly everything else in the state.

It was a fresh start. The sky was the limit.

I unpacked in my room, one of four in a former stand-alone garage converted by our landlady's late husband into private housing for UT students. We shared a bathroom, refrigerator and central air conditioning. Did I mention it was hot?

Then, I took a stroll. The small theater on the "Drag" (a portion of Guadalupe Street that runs along the western edge of the University of Texas campus), featured "The

University of Texas, Austin. / Robert Morton

Last Picture Show", a sex-washed coming of age film about a dying Texas town shot in black and white. It served as a perfect symbol of where I found myself at this point in time, right in the middle of the old-new West and the continental United States. We were at Ground Zero in the "revolution" whereby the Left assumed control of the U.S. media and most college campuses with the Vietnam War, Richard Nixon and Watergate as rallying cries.

Change was afoot even in the great state of Texas where Austin had emerged as a liberal enclave. I met my first new roommate when he pulled up in his dark-red Ford Eldorado semi-pickup. "Hi, I'm John Doss out of Abilene," he said. Short and feisty, he walked with a swagger and sported cowboy boots and shoulder-length hair under his cowboy hat. I was to have many political and philosophical discussions with 'John Doss out of Abilene' and his Jewish girlfriend Jan from San Antonio. Other roommates were Joaquin Castillo, a Mexican American engineering student determined to work in the space industry and Grady Garcia, an effeminate music student.

None of my new Texas friends were practicing Christians raised with prayer and Bible study like friends from my Protestant cultural milieu on the other side of the Mississippi River.

My Grandpa Morton, revered by his family and all who knew him, had ministered to Christian churches from Texas to Virginia, Arkansas and Tennessee. No one recalled hearing him speak a word in anger. My mother's large and happy family, the Hills, were farmers, teachers, doctors and Baptists not necessarily in that order. Both of my parents had survived the Great Depression and served in World War II.[1]

In contrast to this upbringing, my new home in Austin felt like a spiritual desert. But the glorious sunsets and subsequent walks in the unpopulated expanses of the hill country afforded time to meditate, reflect and search for elusive inner truth.

I had graduated three months earlier with a degree in

---

1 My mother was up at dawn, reading her Bible and praying before cooking our breakfast. She read voraciously, never complained and made a lasting-loving impression on the very young children in her Sunday School classes. My father's passion was the theater pipe organs that accompanied the silent movies of his youth. He loved the popular music of his era and played the organ and piano for events his father might have considered worldly. He built our home with his own hands, and we helped him add a new section for the pipes, percussion, blower and pipe organ console from a theater in Columbus, Ohio. His fascination with music and writing only reinforced his adamant policy that his father's values were our family's. Television, the "devil's box" he publicly insisted at one church meeting to my humiliation, was not allowed into our home until the 1960s by which time my brother and I were out of synch with our mesmerized peers. [Ironically, after 2 years in Journalism graduate school, I decided my father had been right all along.]

Mathematics from Milligan College in East Tennessee. It was a pleasant Christian Church-related liberal arts college which provided a good basic education in a beautiful setting. Its most famous graduate was Francis Gary Powers.[2]

With my first cousin Ann Hill's husband, Rod Irvin, and my best friend, Steve Knowles from Pleasant Hill, Calif., I had written a popular satire column for the Milligan College Stampede. Based on that notoriety, I had been elected Secretary of the Student Government for which I had written and published minutes satirizing the boring but (in keeping

---

2   Francis Gary Powers (August 17, 1929 – August 1, 1977) was an American pilot whose Central Intelligence Agency (CIA) U-2 spy plane was shot down while flying a reconnaissance mission in Soviet Union airspace, causing the 1960 U-2 incident. Despite controversy including initial CIA claims that his was a weather plane, his failure to activate devices to destroy the plane and to commit suicide and his public apology while imprisoned in the Soviet Union, his actions were subsequently validated after his debriefing and Congressional hearings. During a speech in March 1964, former CIA Director Allen Dulles said of Powers, «He performed his duty in a very dangerous mission and he performed it well, and I think I know more about that than some of his detractors and critics know, and I am glad to say that to him tonight.

with the times) rebellious meetings. My campaign against a serious candidate who was proposing reforms to the college's disciplinary code was not serious and garnered me a landslide victory. My sole campaign pledge had been to return Morton Salt to the college cafeteria. Leaving that cafeteria one day, a student with long hair approached me in confidence about friends he knew who were knowledgeable in explosives. I promptly swore him to secrecy and assured him he would be the first to know if we wanted to get in touch with his friends. This was to be my first and last foray into politics.

I had done well, graduating with honors and winning a teaching fellowship in Mathematics at the University of Texas where I entered the Ph. D. program. I sold my beloved homemade six-inch reflector telescope (with a mirror I had hand-ground) for $50 to pay the union dues to work construction that summer (1971) in Atlanta. I moved there after graduation with my college newspaper friends John Rohrbaugh and Steve Knowles before we all moved on to graduate schools in Boulder, Colorado and Tallahassee, Florida respectively. By luck of the draw, we all had high draft numbers so the Vietnam War was literally and figuratively half a world away.

Atlanta proved to be a life experience with back-breaking work and lime burns from working in concrete. We lived in a low-end inner-city rental with crimes taking place nearby with some regularity. We showed up at the union hall at 5 a.m. every day and there wasn't always work. When there was, it was hard labor. That experience plus my four years of summer manual labor jobs at the Kingsport (Tennessee) Press book-making plant convinced me that physical work was not my forte.

Having worked hard through my school and college years and achieving "success", I had suddenly realized I didn't know where I was going. My friends were getting married and pursuing serious employment or being drafted for the Vietnam War. My goal in graduate school was to become a professor so that I would finally have disposable time to monitor and properly assimilate the classes (especially the reading lists) that I had done well in but not fully absorbed as I had been working more-or-less full time. I was hungry for that knowledge. To that end, even though I wanted to major in literature, I chose mathematics because it was my best subject.

That of course makes absolutely no sense, but at the time it was my path forward.

So, in Texas, what I was really looking for was some space and the necessary resources to reconcile a world within that was at odds with objective reality in my bubble of time and space. Clearly, I was hungry for knowledge, insight and perspective.

I enjoyed the freedom and having some money in my pocket for the first time. But within weeks, there was no avoiding the sinking realization that I was on the wrong track.

Halfway through my first semester at the University of Texas, I rebelled against proving theorems with mental gymnastics that occupied most of my waking hours. I bewildered my freshmen Calculus student by adding questions on current events to their quizzes. Their answers wouldn't be graded I reassured them, but their education should be grounded in reality as well as abstractions.

My mind followed my heart and first thing I knew, my feet were walking me across campus to the School of Communications. Perhaps for the first time ever a student talked his way into the graduate program in Journalism while enrolled in the PhD program in Mathematics.

Dean Wayne Danielson rebuffed my first try, saying that I would have to start over as an undergraduate. A couple of weeks later, I knocked on the door of Graduate Admissions Director for the School of Mass Communications, Dr. Ernest Sharpe. His focus was Advertising and he had among other things played a role in championing avocados in the marketplace. But, in a long, relaxed discussion we discovered a shared fascination with Richard Milhous Nixon. He had a Dallas Morning News background and was generally conservative. Despite my beard and long hair, I was not really a "hippie." I told him I thought many in my generation were projecting on Nixon their own negative traits. Just as they rebelled against their often-authoritarian Dads, many of whom were World War II veterans and survivors of the Great Depression, they likewise despised Nixon for all the wrong reasons.

Dr. Sharpe must have liked what he heard. He was a kind man and not bound by anal bureaucratic restraints. And he was pragmatic. Suddenly animated, he explained that the graduate program at UT's School of Communications was veering away from traditional journalism training and, thanks to the influence of Stanford University, was placing greater emphasis on quantitative research by graduate students working on their theses and dissertations. Statistical analysis and huge punch card computers were suddenly in vogue. The problem, he explained, was that most of his grad students were literally terrified by Math. His eyes lit up. I could be part of the solution. He picked up the phone and called three members of the admissions committee. Suddenly I was in.

This was indeed a miracle and I doubt that precedent has been repeated. I finished out my semester as a Teaching Assistant in Mathematics and then began a Research Associateship in Dr. Sharpe's office helping graduate students with quantitative research while doing my own research enroute to a master's degree in Mass Communications, Journalism.

I enjoyed the writing and editing classes and veered into cognitive dissonance theory of attitude change as a likely thesis topic. I also began to question the underlying roles of the ego and the psyche in thought processes. I was fascinated by the unconscious mind, recorded my dreams, read Carl Jung ("Psychology and Religion") and returned to the Bible but with an inquiring mind. The lyrics to the rock opera Jesus Christ Superstar led me to question some early basic assumptions about religion and life.[3]

Sometimes, however, I felt totally alone and in the depths of despair. Virtually everything in my surroundings seemed superficial and lacked authenticity and meaning. Since my conversion to Christianity at age 8 by my own initiative, I

---

3 The Album [https://en.wikipedia.org/wiki/Jesus_Christ_Superstar_(album)] was released in 1970 and the rock opera premiered in October 1971. My focus was on the music and the lyrics: https://www.stlyrics.com/j/jesuschristsuperstar.htm

Little Angels, Vienna, 2015 / Social media

had prayed daily before sleeping for God's guidance. But midway through my college years, I had dropped that habit in part because I was getting so little sleep. But I was also questioning all prior assumptions like many of my generation. In Texas, I was a semi-educated secularist caught in a confusing cultural revolution. God was no longer a part of my personal matrix.

One night at a party with friends at a house in East Austin, I had a life-changing experience. I was feeling very sick with a bad headache. I laid my head back on the sofa and closed my eyes. After a brief respite, my eyes opened to a translucent world. I could literally see through everyone there, their thoughts and motivations and their fears. A voice in my mind began to explain to me what I was seeing and provided many of the answers I had been searching for. I assumed that it was Jesus, but I also thought of it as the Spirit of Truth. It was an ecstatic experience, at times hilarious. I was made clearly aware of the basic ridiculousness of the human experience that I was seeing all around me at the party. I was living in an "idiocracy". Significantly, my doubts about a loving God were banished forever by this experience with Divinity. I left that party a changed man, like Charlton Heston in the "Ten Commandments" who returned from seeing the Burning Bush with a new hair style and eyes "high on the road." I felt liberated, deeply-loved and ushered into a profoundly new internal existence for which I will always be grateful.[4]

After that night, I decided my friends in downtown Austin were a distraction. I moved out to a stretch of Hwy 71 toward Johnson City into what had been a cowboy apartment which rented for $75/month. There were maybe half a dozen of these one-room cabins scattered along a semi-circle gravel drive, half a mile down 71 from a combined pecan praline factory and post office. Except for scrub brush and the gently rolling hills extending to the distant horizon, there was nothing else in sight to distract from the glorious sunsets.

In another apartment out there in the middle of nowhere lived a burned-out, former Children of God hippie who gave me a kitten as a housewarming gift on the day I moved in. That first night in our new home, my kitten and I were each stung by scorpions. Out in the wide-open spaces, I read the

---

4   Many years later I learned that a former newspaper colleague in New York had written a book about his own "Encounters with the Divine." His name is Al Guart and the book he wrote was entitled: "Beyond the Sphere." Al had been a Unification Church member and a journalism student and newspaper editor at the City University of New York. He had worked for a year at the New York City Tribune before moving on to a teaching job, leaving the church and later beginning a successful career at the New York Post and CBS News as an investigative reporter. But his earlier experiences with God was burned into his being and he felt compelled to share them decades later through his beautifully-written book.

Bible and meditated every day, often wandering out into the brush wilderness at dawn or dusk. My friends finally caught up with me and when they visited, 'John Doss out of Abilene' said I looked like Jesus.

My most memorable class in Austin had no connection to the University of Texas. It was off campus and called Psycho Cybernetics. I paid for 5 classes and made it through 3. They had a profound impact. The former Presbyterian minister taught "Alpha meditation" or mental yoga. We learned to slow down our mind through breathing to a more intuitive state and to discern auras. One of the first side effects of this training was that occasional bouts of indigestion disappeared forever.

With a renewed interest in the spiritual nature of human beings, I stumbled into another life-changing event. During a lunch break with a secretary who worked for Dr. Sharpe and me, we stopped by a book table near the UT tower on campus. I asked if they had anything about Edgar Cayce. A balding young man, Jonathan Slevin, explained that they had more books back at their "center" and invited me over. I assumed this was some kind of UFO group. But I was "searching."

Almost against my better judgement, I later visited the center. Jonathan proceeded to teach something to me called the Principles of Creation. It explained the core purpose of life and the relationship between God and man, mind and body, spirit and physical, religion and science. It was biblically based. When he finished, I asked if I could see his notes. They were from Young Whi Kim's study guide for the Divine Principle by Sun Myung Moon whose name had not been mentioned. I made photocopies and sent them off to a couple of close undergraduate friends whom I considered serious-minded and underwhelmed by the trappings of academic pursuits we had lampooned in college. Subsequent presentations were on the Fall of Man, the Consummation of History and the Mission of Jesus. I had no doubt that these were coming from what I called the Spirit of Truth.

As we walked through the center, Jonathan showed me a calendar with photos of an "international choir" and a Korean dance troupe called the "Little Angels" which I recognized as having performed a concert at Milligan College. And then he told me there was talk of establishing a newspaper. That last piece of information made me think this group might be relevant.

Such was the chain of events that ushered a math graduate student into an unexpected adventure in 20th century American journalism.

CHAPTER 3

THE 'SIBERIAN JEW SYNDROME'

*What would the ideal world be like? It would certainly
not be a place where people are at odds with and jealous
of each other, begrudging one another's successes, and
becoming sick with envy over other people's happiness.
Instead, it would be a world where the
success of one person would be the success of everyone and the
joy of one person would be the joy of everyone. The pleasures
and joys of one person could be shared by everyone in the
whole world.*
— Sun Myung Moon 1967.5.28

1991

I arrived right on time for the dinner meeting at Sun Myung
Moon's estate in Tarrytown, NY on June 1, 1991. It was a
beautiful, sunny, early summer day and not a soul could be
seen outside the building. When I was ushered into the
dining room it was full, and everyone was already seated.
Surprised and embarrassed I took the lone empty chair two-
thirds of the way down from the head of the table.

We ate in silence, the only sounds being the clatter of
cutlery against plates, in a majestic dining room with wall

murals of the great outdoors. The mood was serious.

Had I been given the wrong time intentionally or in error? The invitation had been cryptic and made no mention of who would be there. Looking around, all were known to me and there were at least three people who had my phone number.

Everyone of any significance in Sun Myung Moon's growing media empire were breaking bread together. Up near the head of the table with the Founder himself were new Washington Times President Dong Moon Joo and Deputy Managing Editor Josette Sheeran Shiner. Across the table from them and at Sun Myung Moon's left were Managing Editor and later Editor in Chief Wes Pruden, General Manager Ron Godwin (former business associate of Rev. Jerry Falwell), Noticias del Mundo President Amb. Philip Sanchez, Segye Ilbo's Dae-O Son (the Times' sister newspaper in Seoul) and elder son Hyo-Jin Moon.

I may never know what had been discussed before my arrival, but it quickly became apparent that this meeting was a rare opportunity for the Founder to connect with the leadership of his media companies and to recognize me as a key editor. I had been the Editor in Chief of the recently suspended, award-winning New York City Tribune.

Sun Myung Moon, deeply sun-tanned from frequent fishing expeditions, talked at length about Ron Godwin, The Times and current events. Then he pointed in my direction.

"Look at his forehead," he said. "He doesn't listen to anyone. And he won't listen to you," he added nodding to the top Washington Times honchos at his left and right.

I was dumbfounded.

In retrospect it occurred to me that this remarkable introduction would be regarded very seriously indeed had it been made in a Northeast Asia setting. It would position me for a very significant role. Here in the politicized culture of a U.S. media group shifting its base to Washington, D.C., it was to have the opposite effect. Nevertheless, all that transpired in the years that followed were the responsibility of me and my colleagues as the Founder did not involve himself in day-to-day operations.

June 1, 1991 at 'East Garden' in Tarrytown, NY. From left, Byung-Ho Kim (President of Segye Times in New York, Dong Moon Joo (President of The Washington Times), Josette Sheeran Shiner (Deputy Managing Editor of The Washington Times), Hyo-Jin Moon, Ron Godwin (General Manager of The Washington Times), Sun Myung Moon, Mrs. Moon (Hak-Ja Han), Wesley Pruden (Managing Editor of The Washington Times), the author, Philip Sanchez (President of Noticias del Mundo), Col. Sang-Kil Han, Dae-O Son, President of Segye Ilbo in Seoul.

Sun Myung Moon praised my professionalism, saying that he had given me "very little training." He commended me to Wes and Josette and repeatedly suggested that we work closely together. To Josette, he made the pointed suggestion that she support me as an elder brother. Would she agree? He asked three times. Her response was muted but presumably agreeable.

Looking down the table at Dong Moon Joo, I saw that he looked stricken, and I was left with the unforgettable mental image of him sitting erect and uncomfortable as if on a sharp object.

After dinner, a group photo was taken. Then Wes and Josette were whisked away in a hired car, back to the airport, the shuttle and safety in the nation's capital. Still stunned and internally exhilarated, I found myself alone with Joo outside on the driveway in front. Sun Myung Moon walked out and joined us. He told me I should do my best to work cooperatively with the Washington Times leadership. He then said that after things settled down, his plan was to revive the New York City Tribune and furthermore to establish newspapers throughout the nation and world.

It was to be my last direct encounter with Sun Myung Moon until a fishing trip with him in Kodiak Alaska along with a few Washington Times editors and reporters seven years later in 1998. By his uncharacteristically subdued tone and manner that evening in Tarrytown, I felt he was communicating more than his words expressed. He was in effect expressing regret for how events had transpired [see Chapter 11] and wanted me to know that he was providing his full support despite intense, internal political winds.

I am now and was then clear about my lack of special qualifications for a major editorial role at The Washington Times. The same, to be sure, could be said of Wes Pruden (a high school graduate with formidable writing skills and news judgement who was socially shy and inclined to leave daily newsroom combat to his managing editor) and Josette Shiner (whose stunning good looks, winning personality and social political brilliance surpassed her editorial chops). Had the three of us been able to work together as the Founder had just suggested, we might have been a formidable team.

It was not to be.

Everyone at that dinner on June 1, 1991, were put on notice by the one who had brought us together and founded The Washington Times. But everyone there also had Free Will, like all descendants of Adam and Eve who had exercised it in disastrous fashion, according to Sun Myung Moon. Indeed, the owner of The Washington Times was an alpha-type male if there ever was one. But as strong and authoritarian a leader as he was, he did not interfere in the realm of individual human responsibility of the leaders in organizations he founded and of his immediate family members. So, his words at that dinner were his suggestion, not a direct order, and were taken as such.

I have met and worked with several media moguls at other news organizations over the years, a few of whom may have felt they were God's representative on Earth. Not one of them has provided as much support and editorial freedom as did Sun Myung Moon. Other former editors at The Washington Times have said the same thing.

But why was the extraordinary June 1, 1991, meeting necessary? Filling major editorial positions at American newspapers was during the twentieth century a sensitive issue. Transferring personnel between affiliated publications would not normally require the ownership's direct involvement. But there was nothing normal about this company or the set of circumstances before and after that dinner in Tarrytown, NY.

Despite the Founder's extraordinary effort on my behalf after his earlier directives had been ignored, I later learned, the response from Washington to the dinner meeting of June 1, 1991, was total silence. No one at the NYC Tribune would have been surprised.

My colleagues and I were well aware that The Washington Times wanted its forerunner in New York to disappear. Neither paper was near profitability, and the Washington share of the subsidy pie for U.S. media operations was 95 percent or greater.

The Times did not view charitably the notable editorial achievements of the New York daily at a fraction of the expense. The fact that the prototypes of The Times had been published in our New York newsroom was of no consequence.

As the Tribune's former Editor in Chief and Vice President, I had helped with the planning and early development of The Washington Times in the early 1980s along with several colleagues, a couple of whom were close friends. After the Tribune published its final edition on Jan. 4, 1991, it was almost as if I had died and gone to the Great Beyond.

Only several weeks after the June 1, 1991 meeting, was I

Lev Navrozov, New York City Tribune

to learn that the Founder had earlier made known his wishes concerning my role at The Times even before learning from my confidential correspondence to him in the weeks after the suspension of the NYC Tribune about the deception that preceded that fateful decision in late 1990. Within days of the delivery of that correspondence, a major shakeup had taken place in the Washington, D.C. hub of Sun Myung Moon's media operations.

Why was I left in the dark about all of those directives which were rumored in the newsroom at The Times and well known in its corridors of power on the upper floors? No one has ever volunteered to me the answer to that question.

In early 1991, I had been reliably informed that Sun Myung Moon's close disciple, Takeru Kamiyama, had been instructed to take care of my family financially after the Tribune's closing and that Dong Moon Joo was to facilitate our move to Washington, DC. In fact, my Korea-born wife was told by several Korean sources that they had heard we were already in D.C. But we never heard directly from any representative of Sun Myung Moon, and when I followed up with Mr. Kamiyama and Mr. Joo, what I had gotten from each was nothing more than a testimony to their own difficult and sacrificial experiences in following the Lord of the Second Advent. In other words, I was on my own.

Marveling at the internecine warfare in Sun Myung Moon's media empire, our close friend Lev Navrozov (Soviet émigré, New York City Tribune columnist and chairman of the Alternative to the New York Times Committee) shared with me a term from his life experience and analysis that characterized the phenomenon that had suspended publication of his beloved newspaper.

What we were seeing, he intoned, was a manifestation of the "Siberian Jew Syndrome." No one despises a Siberian Jew more than another Siberian Jew, he explained.

What an interesting characterization of a phenomenon frequently seen in the marginalized community of those associated with Unification Church publications as well as the much larger U.S. Conservative movement, not to mention influential Christian and Jewish subsets of society. Such groups are regarded as leper colonies by politicians and thought leaders in the United States.

The NYC Tribune was deemed by the Washington-based leadership as too close to the Founder's international (and therefore expensive) vision for the media although no one would ever come right out and say so because to do so would suggest lack of support for that vision. Was there room in a growing media empire for both a powerful political Washington newspaper and a conservative alternative to the New York Times? There was not, despite my arguments to the contrary. But that consensus was sub rosa.

At a private meeting in New York City with top officials of the company's senior management immediately prior to their announcement of the Tribune's fate, my leadership team had confronted them with documentation on the fraudulent reports their New York business team had supplied to justify suspending operations.

While our presentation clearly shocked Col. Bo Hi Pak, Amb. Sang Kook Han (who had replaced Pak as the owner's representatives at The Times) and Dong Moon Joo, it made no impact on the decision they had flown to New York to announce. After all, as Amb. Han explained more than once, snow was in the forecast, and they urgently needed to catch the next shuttle flight back to Washington.

Should conscience, facts, fiduciary responsibility and/or loyalty to the Founder's vision have interrupted this media power play? That is not for me to say. But among those disciples and lieutenants of Sun Myung Moon, it was difficult not to conclude that the foundational Judeo-Christian precepts and high principles upon which his Divine Principle was based were secondary.

Priority one was more down to earth: The subsidy-driven rise of The Washington Times in power-obsessed Washington, DC.

CHAPTER 4

VINCE FOSTER, THE WASHINGTON TIMES AND THE TRUTH

1994

Why are the facts about the death of Clinton White House Deputy Counsel Vince Foster on July 20, 1993, important?

Let's start with the following proposition, privately held by the author: Had The Washington Times forcefully prosecuted the story about the multiple questions surrounding Foster's death, which it indirectly helped launch, it could have established itself as the most powerful news organization in the capital of the Free World. It could have furthermore begun the process of upending the all-powerful consensus of the post-World War II liberal media.

There is no way to prove this proposition of course. However, consider that because the Washington Post aggressively and courageously pursued the Watergate scandal which resulted in the resignation of President Richard Nixon, it was able to overtake the Washington Star in circulation. I would argue that the rumored, deep-seated corruption in the Clinton Administration could only have been brought to light and prosecuted by a thorough examination of the facts surrounding the death of the high-

Fort Marcy Park, 1994. / Robert Morton

est-level White House official serving a U.S. president ever to die due to unnatural causes. Such was not accomplished by President Clinton's impeachment on charges of perjury connected to his sexual relationship with White House Intern Monica Lewinsky.

The controversy about the Vince Foster story started with an award-winning article by Washington Times' investigative reporter Jerry Seper: "Clinton Papers Lifted After Aide's Suicide; Foster's Office Was Secretly Searched Hours After His Body Was Found," on Dec. 20, 1993. The opening paragraph read as follows: "White House officials removed records of business deals between President Clinton, his wife and an Arkansas partnership known as Whitewater Development Corp. from the office of Vincent W. Foster Jr. during two searches after the deputy presidential counsel's suicide, The Washington Times has learned."[1]

---

1   If you search for that article at WashingtonTimes.com, you will not find it as it was pub-

It should be noted that on that day access to the Internet was limited, and cable news had not yet dominated the media scene. Thus, after an Independent Counsel was appointed because of the Washington Times article, the Wall Street Journal observed in an editorial that readers interested in the Whitewater scandal would have to subscribe to The Washington Times because no other newspaper was covering it.

It was the sudden national demand for The Washington Times which led to the launching of the Washington Times National Weekly Edition on the 50th anniversary of D-Day, June 6, 1994. I was the first editor of that publication (after first suggesting the concept two years earlier) and continued to serve as such until Jan. 4, 2012, 22 years to the day that the New York City Tribune published its final edition[2].

On Jan. 10, 1994, I had lunch with Editor in Chief Wes Pruden to discuss plans to launch the new publication. It was a cordial occasion during which we sought to ease the strains in a professional relationship caused by the quiet power struggle at the top levels of The Washington Times over my role at the newspaper following the closing of the New York City Tribune, my farewell letter to the Founder and the subsequent meeting with him and his media group's top executives in Tarrytown, NY on June 1, 1991 (See Chapter 3).

Pruden was God's gift to The Times at that point in American history because he was a native of Arkansas and well acquainted with the unique political culture from which

---

lished in the days before the newspaper's Internet edition.

2 See Chapters 5 and 11.

sprang President William Jefferson Clinton. The conversation at lunch turned to Vince Foster. Pruden confided that a coroner in Little Rock with first-hand knowledge said that the state of Foster's body when it was discovered did not support the official finding that he committed suicide. For me there were two takeaways from this conversation: 1) There were significant questions about how Vince Foster died and 2) The Washington Times had no intention of answering such questions.

Wes Pruden, who was still working as a top editor at the Washington Times when he died on July 17, 2019, was nothing if not a survivor. I often thought of him as like the ancient catfish in a lake in the Deep South that never got caught. Throughout his years as president at The Washington Times, Dong Moon Joo sought continuously but unsuccessfully to replace Pruden who was resolute, respectful and unshakable. Wes was also very wise in the ways of Washington. Story selections at The Times reflected his instincts that a conservative newspaper in a liberal Democrat city, that had the additional distinction of being founded by a man considered by his followers to be the Messiah, should pick its fights with great care.

A few days after my lunch with Pruden, Chris Ruddy (who would later establish Newsmax Media) called me from New York. After the suspension of the New York City Tribune and its Long Island edition, published with the assistance of Ruddy and his contacts [See Chapter 11], he had launched the New York Guardian weekly. One of his articles came to the attention of Rupert Murdoch at the New York Post who had directed that Ruddy be brought on as a contract reporter.

"Are there any stories in Washington I could pursue?" Ruddy inquired.

"You should take a look at Vince Foster," I responded. "People here are talking about him, but no one is writing about him."

By Jan. 20, Ruddy had checked in at the Key Bridge Marriott Hotel. He invited me to join him at an interview he had set up with the paramedic in Fairfax County Virginia who had discovered Foster's body in Fort Marcy Park. This Civil War landmark was located just off the George Washington Memorial Parkway, 1/2 mile from the Potomac River on the south side of the Chain Bridge Road leading from Chain Bridge to Langley and McLean, Virginia by way of the nearby CIA Headquarters.

We agreed that he would follow me in his rental car to my home in Falls Church, Virginia. As we left Washington, it was snowing hard and by the time we made it home there was heavy accumulation. Checking in by phone with our source, the lead paramedic of the Fairfax County Fire and Rescue Station No. 1, Ruddy got some disturbing news. A close relation had just died in an auto accident in Long Island, New York. By now it was night. As it continued to snow, we waited, hoping for the opportunity to at least talk with him by phone. Perhaps an hour later, Sgt. George Gonzalez called back and said he wanted to meet. When we joined him at a Chinese takeout restaurant just off Leesburg Pike in Falls Church, it was clear that this man wanted to get something off his chest.

As the snow continued to fall, he described what he had seen at Fort Marcy Park, drawing diagrams and a map on

WHAT I SAW AT THE SECOND COMING...

napkins. Two memories from that night stand out. First, Chris Ruddy, who has always had a hearty appetite was suffering from severe indigestion. (He later wondered whether he had suffered food poisoning at the Key Bridge Marriott.) That did not stop him from a careful line of questioning which reminded me that he was the son of a New York City police detective.

Secondly, at the end of the interview, the Fairfax County officer asked if we had any additional questions. I said, "You must have dealt with the press in your job." He said that yes, he had dealt with murders and suicides and had often been approached by the media. "How many reporters have you spoken with about Vince Foster's death?" I asked.

"You guys are the first," he responded.

I was stunned. We were speaking six months almost to the day after he had responded to the report of a body in the park that happened to be one of the highest-level White House officials ever to die while working there.

On Jan. 27, 1994, Ruddy's first article appeared in the New York Post: "Doubts Raised over Foster's 'Suicide'".

The rest, as they say is history. The National Weekly Edition of The Washington Times began publication some six months later and carried the results of Ruddy's lengthy investigation, first at the NY Post, then at the Pittsburgh Tribune Review, but only in the form of full-page advertisements sponsored by Joseph Farah's Western Journalism Foundation. The Washington Times, as I had correctly surmised, was not going to touch that story.

Ruddy's book, "The Strange Death of Vincent Foster," may not be a work that he now wants to call attention to.

As founder of Newsmax, he has made peace with Bill and Hillary Clinton and a photo of Bill's visit to Newsmax is (or was when I worked there as Associate Editor) given prominent display at the Newsmax offices in West Palm Beach, Florida.

The final paragraph of that book, to my mind, perfectly sums up the significance of the Vince Foster mystery:

> A visit to Fort Marcy Park — built on President Lincoln's orders — takes one back to a critical period in our history when rivers of blood were spilled in order to preserve this unique experiment of ours — this government where justice would reign supreme, and no man, no group of men, no matter how powerful or highly placed, would be exempt from public accountability. With the "investigations" of the Park Police, the FBI, Fiske, and Starr, this tiny square of land may yet become the symbol of a cover-up by people who have, with the help of the press, placed themselves above the law.

CHAPTER 5

'START SPREADING THE NEWS' — NEW YORK, NEW YORK

Start spreading the news
I'm leaving today
I want to be a part of it
New York, New York ...

If I can make it there
I'll make it anywhere
It's up to you
New York, New York

New York, New York — Frank Sinatra
Songwriters: John Kander / Fred Ebb

1976-1990

If Sun Myung Moon's media empire had made it in New York, where it began, perhaps it could have made it anywhere.

Didn't happen.

The consensus reached by his lieutenants in the 1980s was to focus all publishing efforts and resources in Washington,

DC. That policy, never endorsed by Sun Myung Moon himself, was popular with the rank and file of American Unification Church members and was based on the logic that there simply was not enough money to support two money-losing newspapers. In addition, the lifestyle options in the Washington, DC metropolitan area were more attractive for young people with families.[1]

All of which raises the question: What did the Founder want?

When Sun Myung Moon expanded his focus from Korea and Japan to America in the 1970s, his plan was to establish worldwide missions intended to take root and flourish. Clearly, he would also leverage support from the then-respected Christian West for the unification of his divided homeland of Korea as the nexus of the Kingdom of God on Earth.

Two cities, Washington, DC and New York City, were bases for early missionary activity. Where would he establish headquarters and install a spiritual and material infrastructure to secure and nurture his expanding membership and his growing family?

He chose the latter, the first capital of the United States.

---

1 See Chapter 2, of the author's 1977 master's degree thesis at the University of Texas at Austin: "But what is most damaging to the city's economy is the exodus of large business firms from New York to other major American cities or to outlying suburban areas. ... Many a company will have a difficult time attracting talented employees because they simply don't want to move their families to New York." Included in the book, "The News World of New York City: A Retrospective," 2023, Origin 2021 Publishing.

New York City in 1976 was the cultural and financial hub for America's most productive and talented people. From Broadway to the twin towers in Wall Street, Manhattan was a tourist mecca for Americans wanting to see the world without leaving the country.

The Unification Church purchased a building on 4 West 43rd St. as its national headquarters and the New Yorker Hotel on 34th St. and Eighth Ave. to house hundreds of young members who arrived to "restore" a sinful city. Both buildings were walking distance from Times Square, the New York Times, the Empire State Building and Macy's.

Sun Myung Moon spoke early each Sunday morning at the much more idyllic Belvedere Estates in Tarrytown in Westchester County to hundreds of followers on the sprawling grounds overlooking the Hudson River. His "East Garden" residence nearby hosted leaders conferences and other smaller gatherings.

For those pioneering Sun Myung Moon's first newspaper in America, New York City was a cold, dirty and forbidding landscape dominated by leftwing political forces, powerful newspapers and newspaper unions and a highly diverse population scrambling for survival and triumph in the "city that never sleeps."

On the last day of 1976, the New York News World published its first daily edition from the 11th floor of the recently purchased New Yorker Hotel. In the spirit of "restoring" the media, the staff had first repaired, cleaned and painted the rundown hotel rooms which served as the first newsroom. A few weeks later, the operation moved several blocks East to the Tiffany building at 401 Fifth Ave.[2] where the third-floor newsroom actually looked like a newsroom. In fact, movie director Oliver Stone once came over in the 1980s, visited my corner office, and checked us out as a potential newsroom setting for his 1987 film "Wall Street".

The newspaper business in the 1970s was an exciting prospect for young idealistic and ambitious Americans committed to changing the world. But Sun Myung Moon expected everyone to build their careers from the ground up. This included delivering early morning newspaper home delivery routes throughout the city including the most run-down parts of Harlem where I went daily despite late night deadlines. I recall while collecting subscription fees on a Saturday morning being invited inside an apartment where the family was gathered in the kitchen around the gas range to stay warm because the building's radiators were not working.

Getting that first edition of the newspaper out on December 30, 1976, was war. Veteran newspaper men and women were later hired for the City Desk, Sports Desk and Copy Desk to enhance professional standards for a staff that had been assembled in less than two months. But the typesetting machines had arrived only days before launch in the last week of 1976.[3] Typeset copy and headline strips were waxed and "pasted" on to the pages which were then photographed and burned onto plates for the presses. One early memory of the chaos was a headline writer sprinting down the hotel hallway, with a strip of headlines trailing behind him as deadlines loomed.

---

2   Ibid, Chapters 4,5.
3   Ibid.

The News World successfully launched and never missed a day including the New York City blackout of 1977 and the newspaper strike in 1978. As documented below, it broke many exclusives.

As the critical election of 1980 approached, I as the editor, astounded my senior editors by taking time off to collaborate on an eight-part series with News Editor Ted Agres, "Subversion in Washington: The Radical Network That's Infiltrated The White House."

That series exposed the extent to which pro-Soviet communist front groups had penetrated policy and media institutions in the nation's capital. It also introduced me to key players in Washington's coming Reagan era including the group of former generals who pioneered the Strategic Defense Initiative which arguably helped win the Cold War against the Soviet Union.

One of them, Gen. Robert Richardson, introduced me to his friend and former CIA counterintelligence legend James Jesus Angleton whom I would later introduce to a new hire and future Washington Times star reporter Bill Gertz.

One article in that series involved my translating into nonfiction a spy novel by Arnaud de Borchgrave and Robert Moss, "The Spike." This article caused consternation for Arnaud because as he explained to me, the book was written as fiction for a reason, given the sinister and litigious forces and personalities it depicted. Arnaud, who would later become Editor in Chief at The Washington Times, later told me he was in my debt for putting him on the radar screen of the newspaper's senior management.

The New York Tribune later replaced the New York News

State of New York - Department of State

Certificate of Trade-Mark Registration

I, GAIL S. SHAFFER, SECRETARY OF STATE OF THE STATE OF NEW

YORK, do hereby CERTIFY that in accordance with the application filed in this office on

the __21st__ day of __December__ ,19 82 , the TRADEMARK described

below has been duly registered in this Department pursuant to Article 24 of the General Business

Law, in behalf of NEWS WORLD COMMUNICATIONS, INC. (New York Corp.)
_____Name_____

401 Fifth Avenue, New York, New York 10016
_____Address_____

Description of Trademark and Description of Goods on Which the Trademark is Used:

"THE NEW YORK TRIBUNE"

Used in connection with newspapers.

The New York Tribune

Class of Merchandise: No. 38		File No. R-21407
Date of Registration: 1-11-83		Registration Expires: 1-11-93
Date First Used In UNITED STATES: 12/17/82		
Date First Used In NEW YORK STATE: 12/17/82		

WITNESS my hand and the seal of the Department
of State at the City of Albany, this __11th__
day of __January__ 19 83

_____
Secretary of State

The Trademark Registration for The New York Tribune was signed by Sun Myung Moon. / Robert Morton

World which had been modeled after its counterpart in Tokyo, Sekai Nippo. After a bitter internal dispute in 1980-82 over positioning and format, my understanding of the Founder's intent was confirmed. It was to be a serious broadsheet metropolitan daily newspaper, not a tabloid, and was intended to offer an alternative to the New York Times, not to the New York Daily News or the New York Post.

In an author's note for my book "The News World of New

70th Birthday Tribute

Reverend Sun Myung Moon
Founder
New York City Tribune

York City: A Retrospective", I wrote the following:

The News World of New York City published its first edition on the last day of 1976 as an alternative to the New York Times and as the first daily newspaper in a publishing company that would later include The Washington Times.

The last serious broadsheet newspaper competing with the New York Times had been the New York Herald Tribune which ceased publication on April 24, 1966. As a left-leaning "Newspaper of Record," the New York Times had been unchallenged in the marketplace of ideas as the dominant influence on the national media including television and on U.S. politics and culture.

As a founding member of the editorial team at The News World, which was renamed the New York City Tribune in 1983, the author wrote this volume in 1977 as a thesis for his Master's Degree in Journalism from the University of Texas at Austin. His thesis committee recommended that he proceed from the unique vantage point of "Participant-Observer as Pediatric Historian". The Thesis was titled: "The Making of a New Metropolitan Daily in New York: The News World".

In addition to chronicling the newspaper's launch, the thesis examined media trends and factors responsible for newspaper successes and failures in that era. It also compared The News World with the New York Times and the Christian Science Monitor. All three newspapers featured editorial idealism and character that traced to organized religion. The Times was established by a tightly-knit Jewish family, the Christian Science Monitor was inspired the Christian Science Church of Mary Baker Eddy, and The News World was founded by Rev. Sun Myung Moon who was considered by many of his followers to be the returning Messiah.

The brief life of The News World (1976-1983) followed by the Tribune (1983-Jan. 4, 1991) preceded The Washington Times and the advent of cable news and the Internet media revolution. Its issues are on microfilm, and all printed editions are in storage.

I served as the Tribune's Editor in Chief from 1983 until its 1991 suspension working from an office that overlooked Fifth Avenue.

The New York Tribune changed its name again to New York City Tribune after the New York Times claimed it owned our name having acquired the assets of its defeated rival, the New York Herald Tribune after its final edition on April 24, 1966. Those assets it said included the name of both the former New York Tribune and the former New York Herald.[4] In an ornate room at the International Herald Tribune where I went to sign the legal settlement with the New York Times, I saw a very few framed remnants of these New York dailies that had lost the great war of ideas in their death struggle with the "Old Gray Lady", the pro-communist and anti-conservative "newspaper of record."

Earlier, I had contacted famed attorney Alan Dershowitz and asked if he would represent us pro bono against the New York Times on First Amendment grounds. He enthusiastically agreed. However, Sun Myung Moon's chief media lieutenant, Bo Hi Pak declined the offer. I had argued that

---

4 Ibid, Chapter 2.

the legal battle would be a bonanza in terms of free publicity and promotions.

Pak made clear to subordinates that he wanted no distractions or competition from New York with The Washington Times. Ultimately, that unwritten policy proved fatal not only to the New York newspaper but arguably to the Founder's vision for an international media network with a hub in every nation [see Chapters 8, 9 and 11].

What follows are photos and copies of pages from a report about the New York City Tribune that was presented to its Founder, Sun Myung Moon, on his 70th birthday. That tribute serves as both a historical record and an offering on behalf of the many who sacrificed their youth, and in a few cases their lives, to finance and publish this newspaper.

THE CITY OF NEW YORK
OFFICE OF THE MAYOR
NEW YORK, N.Y. 10007

May 20, 1988

Robert J. Morton
Editor in Chief
New York City Tribune
c/o New York Hilton
New York, New York

Dear Bob:

On behalf of the City of New York, I am pleased to extend greetings to the readers and friends of the New York City Tribune on the occasion of tonight's salute from the East Side Conservative Club.

The Tribune has established itself as an articulate and effective voice in New York, thereby strengthening our city's reputation as a center of publishing and communications. The Tribune offers New Yorkers a unique and outspoken viewpoint on the news, and helps to assure that all points of view are represented on the city's newstands.

My best wishes to everyone attending for a most successful and enjoyable evening.

Sincerely,

Edward I. Koch
Mayor

NEW YORK CITY TRIBUNE BUILDING
HEADQUARTERS OF NEWS WORLD COMMUNICATIONS, INC.

New York City Tribune

Rising to the Challenge of The Times

January 6, 1990

Dear Reader,

The *New York City Tribune* exists for a simple reason.

The *New York Times* is a political and cultural monopoly that must be challenged by journalists and columnists who know what New Yorkers have been missing.

The notion of the *New York Times* as **the** "newspaper of record" and an unchallenged cultural arbiter in a city as powerful and diverse as New York, contradicts the democratic foundations on which this nation was established.

New York is, after all, the preeminent American city.

It has been the port of entry for millions of immigrants who have swelled the human resources of these United States.

New York is, furthermore, the financial capital of the nation. Let it not be forgotten that our first president was inaugurated on Wall Street.

The often exhilarating, often frustrating challenges of life in "the City" stem in large part from its very diversity. Homogeneous communities achieve harmony more easily. In what other city is the stage being set for the coming "global village?"

And yet New York has come to be regarded as somehow a foreign city at odds with the rest of the nation. The "imperial *Times*" must share responsibility for this misperception.

In 1976, when this newspaper published its first edition, the *Times* had eliminated its last major competitor, *The New York Herald Tribune*, and was confronted only by two money-losing tabloid newspapers which have never attained either the influence or the major advertising accounts controlled by the *Times*.

At a time when newspaper believability in the eyes of the American public has declined to an all-time low, according to recent Gallup polls, the *New York City Tribune* has appeared on the scene. It has fought to establish an independent point of view, to avoid falling into the trap of "pack journalism," and to challenge what Arnaud de Borchgrave of *The Washington Times* calls the "dominant media culture."

I would offer that this independent point of view, grounded in the family values of our nation's founding Judaeo-Christian tradition, is a superior one. It is one shaped by the columnists and staff of this newspaper, whose backgrounds and achievements are outlined in the following pages.

Without the founding spirit and financial backing of the Reverend Sun Myung Moon over the past 13 years, their reporting and commentary would in effect have been censored — a tragic paradox for such a great and free City.

Above all — as our Publisher Ambassador Phillip Sanchez emphasizes — the *New York City Tribune* seeks to revive the notion of a newspaper as public servant by seeking to provide an alternative source of information to enable New Yorkers to make up their own minds.

We need your help. Yes, buy the *New York City Tribune* and advertise in its pages. But also please be an active participant in our editorial process. Call us about errors, tip us off about significant stories, and submit letters to the editor and commentaries.

We can rise to the challenge of the times by reviving the idea of mass communications as a two-way street in which the truth prevails in the free marketplace of ideas.

Thank you and may God bless your family in this exciting new decade!

Sincerely Yours,

Robert J. Morton
Editor in Chief

New York City Tribune

From a
Proud Tradition

A new era of modern journalism began on Dec. 31, 1976 — the last day of America's bicentennial. On that day, *The News World* (the precursor to today's *New York City Tribune*) was launched, and although few realized it at the time, it was the beginning of a unique and important media group which was to include *Free Press International, Noticias del Mundo, The Washington Times,* and *Insight* and *World & I* magazines.

Since its inception, the *New York City Tribune* has had its moments of glory. During the blackout of 1977, it was the only newspaper to publish, with reporters working by candlelight to write and edit stories before sending them to an upstate printing plant. One year later, when a strike shut down the City's other major dailies, this newspaper continued to publish, with its circulation soaring to nearly 400,000 daily. Several striking reporters and editors from *The New York Times*, the *Post* and the *Daily*

News found temporary employment with the paper during those three months.

In the 1980s the *New York City Tribune* broke numerous important stories that the major media either missed or picked up later. In-depth reports detailed how left-wing organizations bent on dismantling this country's intelligence and military structures infiltrated the policy-

making apparatus of the Carter administration; an investigative report spotlighted the shady real estate dealings of Democratic vice presidential candidate Geraldine Ferraro and her husband John Zaccaro, prompting a series of media investigations that helped thwart Democratic Party hopes in 1984; a series exposed how the Soviet Union used a major department at the United Nations as its

New York City Tribune

From a Proud Tradition

"fiefdom" and as a base for intelligence operations in this country; and an article about a federally funded work of "art" featuring a crucifix submerged in the artist's urine caught the attention of columnist and commentator Patrick Buchanan and generated a national furor.

Through the turbulence of the 1980s, the *New York City Tribune* featured refugee and emigre reports calling attention to the realities of life behind the Iron Curtain, documented the shifting balance of power and the consequences to the geopolitical confrontation between East and West, revealed Soviet motivations behind the invasion of Afghanistan and the political maneuverings surrounding the confirmation of the INF treaty,

and reported firsthand the upheavals within the Soviet empire that resulted in the stunning events that swept through Eastern Europe in late 1989.

The burgeoning, organized crime-linked pornography industry, bias in the major media, the City's unsuccessful attempt to locate a "needle center" for addicts near a public school in Chelsea were among the other stories the *New York City Tribune* covered exclusively for its readers.

The widely-aclaimed Commentary section, which Mayor Koch called the "best in the nation," regularly featured views and opinions otherwise unavailable for serious-minded New Yorkers.

Clockwise from far left: President-elect Ronald Reagan holds up *The News World* edition predicting his 1980 landslide victory; a young Nicaraguan refugee. News editor Evans Johnson; former Mayor Koch catches up on the news. News World Communications President Dr. Bo Hi Pak congratulates Ronald Reagan on his 1980 victory; the *New York City Tribune* newsroom; the same newsroom during the blackout of 1977; some 800 New Yorkers at the Hilton Hotel where the East Side Conservative Club paid tribute to the *New York City Tribune* in 1988.

New York City Tribune

From a Proud Tradition

JESSE HELMS,
U.S. Senator, North Carolina
"The *New York City Tribune* has the unfailing courage to tell the truth and an unyielding willingness to stand up for principles that deserve to survive.
"I not only congratulate all who have had a hand in the success of your paper, but I am grateful to you for daring to be different in an era of knee-jerk, copy-cat journalism. The *City Tribune* has made a difference and America is better off for it."

EDWARD I. KOCH,
former mayor, New York City
"For the last five year I had the pleasure of being a weekly columnist for the *New York City Tribune*. What makes this newspaper's pages so unique is the abundance of commentary on the full range of issues and problems which confront our City and our country. Oftentimes the subject of these commentaries was the work of my administration. Whether criticized or praised, your commentaries helped make me a better mayor."

CHARLES M. LICHENSTEIN,
Senior Fellow, Heritage Foundation
"The *New York City Tribune* displays its values — the fundamental affirmations of family and country, and of the primacy of freedom as the organizing principle of human society — openly and with unapologetic pride. And it restores some luster, in scarce supply these days to the concept of professionalism in the practice of journalism."

ARNAUD DE BORCHGRAVE,
Editor in Chief, The Washington Times
"You are to be commended for your unique contribution in the war of ideas. Yours is now the only truly alternative voice in the great city of New York."

HERB LONDON,
Dean, Gallatin Division,
New York University
"Let it be noted that the *New York City Tribune* is the alternative to the mainstream press. This newspaper has been able to break the stories that do not appear elsewhere. For serious students of politics, economics and culture, this newspaper is indispensible and has come to serve as a model for what journalists and journalism should be."

SERPHIN R. MALTESE,
Chairman,
New York State Conservative Party
"Pro-American, pro-freedom, pro-free enterprise, pro-family, pro-morality! And in the heart of liberaldom! "Thank God for the existence of the *New York City Tribune*."

Major Awards

National Press Club

★ *1984 National 1st Place Award.*
An investigative series by *Karen Shelton* and *John Richardson* detailed reasons for the decline of the New York subway system and compared it with similar systems in other world capitals.

★ *1979 Vivian Award for Meritorius Service.* — *Josette Sheeran*

Investigative Reporters and Editors

★ *1985 National 1st Place Award.*
An investigative series by *Peter Klebnikov* revealed extensive links between Democratic vice presidential candidate Geraldine Ferraro's and her husband's real estate firm and a building they owned and managed that housed a major organized crime-linked distributor of hardcore pornographic publications.

New York Press Club

★ *1978 Cub Reporter of the Year* — *Cheryl Smith*
★ *1981 Cub Reporter of the Year* — *Doug Ashley*
★ *1982 Cub Reporter of the Year* — *Kate Cahill*
★ *1983 Cub Reporter of the Year* — *Mark Palmer*
★ *1984 Cub Reporter of the Year* — *Karen Nelis*
★ *1983 Heart of New York Award* — *Cheryl Smith*
★ *1984 1st Place Feature Photography Award* — *Michael Jones*
★ *1985 1st Place Feature Photography Award* — *Maria Bastone*
★ *1986 Honorable Mention Spot News Photography* — *Jose Rivera*
★ *1989 1st Place Feature Photography Award* — *Mitsu Yasukawa*

New York State Editors Association

★ *1984 1st Place Investigative Reporting Award* — *Karen Shelton*

Silurian Society

★ *1978 1st Place Feature Photography Award* — *Doug Weitzstein*
★ *1981 Honorable Mention for Distinguished Reporting* — *Cheryl Smith*
★ *1982 1st Place Feature Photography Award* — *Vicki Sheeran*
★ *1983 1st Place Feature Photography Award* — *Carol Van Jinbo*
★ *1985 Honorable Mention Feature Photography* — *Chris Gierlich*
★ *1989 1st Place Feature Photography Award* — *Mitsu Yasukawa*

Sigma Delta Chi

★ *1984 1st Place Feature Photography Award* — *Michael Jones*

Newspaper Guild

★ *1978 Page One Award for News Photo* — *Vicki Sheeran*

National Clarion Award for Women in Communications

★ *1980 Honorable Mention* — *Cheryl Smith*

New York City Patrolman's Association

★ *1984 Award for Crime Reporting* — *Chet Marchwinski*

New York City Tribune

The 1980s A Decade of Exclusives

1980

April 25: — Pentagon officials, in a special report, warned that U.S. defenses were stretched dangerously thin. "Today we are trying to meet a three-ocean requirement with a one-and-a-half ocean Navy," said Chief of Naval Operations Adm. Thomas D. Hayward.

"The first thing we need to enunciate is a clear U.S. national strategy against which military proposals could be judged," said retired Lt. Gen. Daniel Graham, former director of the Defense Intelligence Agency. "We have been without a viable and even describable U.S. strategy since the mid-1960s."

Aug. 26: Jimmy Carter's brother Billy was a key element in a broad strategy by the radical government in Libya to influence U.S. foreign policy, intelligence officials told a panel of senators in a closed session.

David Aaron: Couldn't keep secrets.

Oct. 28: WASHINGTON — A special investigation shed light on a network of left-wing organizations in Washington that crusaded for the dismantling of existing U.S. intelligence and military structures and contributed substantially to the formation of policy under the Carter administration.

At the hub of an interlocking conglomerate of "progressive" organizations was the Institute for Policy Studies (IPS) with headquarters just off Dupont Circle.

The eight-part series revealed the following:

● David L. Aaron, President Carter's deputy national security adviser, leaked information about the existence of "stealth" technology and disclosed to a *Newsweek* correspondent the existence of a CIA mole in the Soviet Foreign Ministry, intelligence sources confirmed. Aaron had formerly served as a consultant for the Center for International Policy, an IPS cousin.

● National Security Council member Robert Pastor had collaborated with the IPS on a U.S. policy toward Latin America that focused on strict human rights standards for all Latin American nations except Cuba.

Ronald Reagan: Landslide win predicted.

● A direct effort by the late chairman of the Joint Chiefs of Staff to oust Carter's Latin America specialist on the National Security Council was thwarted because, as Aaron told Secretary of Defense Harold Brown, the specialist — Robert Pastor — was protected "behind Rosalyn Carter's skirts."

Nov. 4: In a historic issue the *New York City Tribune* predicted Ronald Reagan's landslide victory stating he would garner more than 350 electoral votes and carry New York as well.

1981

March 2: Senior U.S. officials confirmed intelligence reports that communist arms shipments to leftist guerrillas in El Salvador were escalating and expressed concern that the American media would be used to oppose U.S. interests in the region.

March 3: In an interview with the *New York City Tribune*, Russian emigre Lev Navrozov stated that *The New York Times'* incomplete and biased coverage of the Soviet Union was not so much a result of Soviet disinformation or penetration by agents as much as an operating mindset that promoted reportorial laziness.

An independent press is crucial for the survival of democracy, Navrozov went on to say. "A two-party system with one newspaper doesn't work."

March 14: Mahmet Ali Agca, who attempted to assassinate Pope John Paul II, was linked to international terrorist organizations. Other media reports had described Agca as a Turkish criminal with rightist associations. However, New York-based terrorism experts hypothesized that Agca was being used as a tool by the Soviet Union to stop the increasingly powerful Polish labor movement.

Mehmet Ali Agca: No rightist after all.

March 18: SAN SALVADOR, El Salvador — President Jose Napoleon Duarte told the *New York City Tribune* that before the Reagan administration sounded the alarm about communist infiltration and subversion in Central America, no one took the threat seriously. "For the whole year, we've been talking about foreign infiltration. The media wouldn't listen. There was no news."

June 8: More than 120 writers, correspondents, columnists and reporters gathered on June 3 at the Waldorf-Astoria to participate in the first meeting of the "Alternative to *The New York Times* Committee, chaired by Lev Navrozov.

One writer told Navrozov that he had submitted an article on the conference and it had been "spiked" (not published).

Navrozov had challenged editors and columnists from *The New York Times* to appear at the meeting for a debate. Although two administrative staff members and one reporter from the *Times* were seen at the meeting, no representative of the *Times* registered.

Consequently, Navrozov branded the authorities at the *Times* as "moral cowards." He also termed the *Times* an "overwhelming cultural and political monopoly."

July 27: A secret meeting in Hyannis, Mass., of activists and wealthy donors in organizations opposed to new religions was covered by an editor, a reporter and a photographer from the *New York City Tribune*. The conferees, taken off-guard by the unexpected attention, hid their faces from the photographer and sought to escape the conference room out a rear exit. All three journalists were assaulted by conference organizers, Edward Levine, a professor at Loyola University in Chicago, tried to smash the camera of photographer Vicky Sheeran. "You're lucky you're a broad," he said. "I'm not a broad, I'm a woman," she replied. "You're a broad," the sociology professor insisted.

William S. Coffin: Uncharitable host.

Oct. 11: The *New York City Tribune's* managing editor, a reporter and a photographer were assaulted and ejected while trying to cover a conference in support of African revolutionary movements hosted by the Riverside Church. Senior minister William Sloan Coffin had opened the meeting with greetings and Rep. George Crockett, D-Michigan, had delivered the keynote address in which he quoted a statement by Fidel Castro that the "core of the (Reagan) administration is fascist." Managing editor Jonathan Slevin was assaulted after asking the conference coordinator for a statement on the Afghan freedom fighters.

Dec. 14: A City public high school near Grammercy Park was found to be the site of a Marxist "tribunal" on "U.S. war crimes against the people of the world" at which the overthrow of the U.S. government was advocated.

One week earlier school facilities were used by the Association of Arab-American University Graduates. Rabbi Seymour Siegel, president of the American Jewish Forum, said in an interview that the association was "pro-PLO, which means they're pro-Soviet Union.... To use our public schools to launch a demonstration which is obviously anti-Jewish or anti any group is something I feel should not be allowed."

1982

March 9: BONN, West Germany — A special report detailed the extent of Soviet support for the "peace movement" in Western Europe. According to a State Department report, a Soviet ambassador tried to bribe the commerce minister of a Western European nation with cheaper oil in exchange for opposition to nuclear modernization.

March 15: TOKYO — A private think tank here disclosed the agenda of Chinese Premier Zhao Ziyang during his visit to North Korea in late 1981. "Zhao complained about Pyongyang's inadequate control of the population along North Korea's border with China and about North Korean attempts to interfere" in the region, said

New York City Tribune

The 1980s
A Decade of
Exclusives

Kinji Yajima of the Studies Center for International Affairs. "He also warned North Korea not to stage an invasion of South Korea to divert attention from its internal troubles."

Oct. 1: Former Black Panther leader Eldridge Cleaver announced to Columbia University students that he had rejected communism and that the United States, despite its problems, offered the most freedom of any nation in the world. "I've done a full circle, and I submit that we need a new consensus of stability in our democracy — we don't need to destroy the whole system."

1983

Jan. 18: A Romanian defector and former pilot, George Hirsovescu, told the *New York City Tribune* Romania has trained Angolans in guerrilla warfare since 1979. He said he flew the guerrillas every three or four months between military aviation schools in Bucharest and guerrilla bases in Angola. He also flew many shipments of weapons to locations throughout Africa.

Oct. 27: WASHINGTON — Mideast experts in Washington said it would be disastrous for the United States to pull its Marines out of Lebanon in the aftermath of the assault on the Marine compound that left 241 dead, as it would open the door for vastly increased Syrian influence in Lebanon.

1984

Jan. 16: Western intelligence agencies were so alarmed by reports of KGB complicity in the assassination attempt on Pope John Paul II that they issued a rash of leaks to *The New York Times* and other media outlets to cover its evidence, said journalist Claire Sterling. The leaks portrayed the attempt on the pope's life as the work of a lone religious fanatic rather than a plot supported by the Bulgarian Intelligence Service and the KGB, she told the Overseas Press Club. Sterling had just published a book, *The Time of the Assassins*, on the assassination conspiracy.

Eldridge Cleaver: Renounced communism.

Jan. 23: A former KGB officer who defected while based in Tokyo told the *New York City Tribune* that his revelations, as published in John Baron's book, *The Hidden Hand*, had succeeded in destroying the KGB's network of Japanese informers. One such agent, the editor in chief of the only major conservative daily in Tokyo — *Sankei Shimbun* — resigned his position but never confessed to any wrongdoing. Most of the other agents he exposed kept their former positions because Japan has no anti-espionage laws with which to prosecute them, he said.

Jan. 24: A four-part series explored the utilization of the 680 Soviets in New York City, most of which are posted at the United Nations, and an estimated one-third of which are intelligence agents.

Sources said that the PSCA was virtually a "Soviet fiefdom," which was used to good effect to manipulate the agenda to fit Moscow's needs.

Non-Soviet civil servants in the PSCA who did not bend to the will of Undersecretary General Viacheslav Ustinov could not look forward to advancement in their careers.

The U.N. also served as an important source of foreign exchange for the Soviets, providing an estimated $22.7 million annually. According to analysis, the average salary of the 432 Soviet employees at the United Nations was $52,571. According to FBI sources, no Soviet employee retained his salary.

Feb. 21: One week after Konstantin Chernenko succeeded Yuri Andropov as leader of the Soviet Communist Party, the *New York City Tribune* reported that 52-year-old Mikhail S. Gorbachev had delivered a major speech at the Central Committee meeting called on Feb. 13 to approve Chernenko's selection. The report also noted that Gorbachev took a senior position in ranking, standing at Chernenko's right at Andropov's graveside.

Mikhail Gorbachev: Destined to succeed.

June 11: WASHINGTON — Twenty-five percent of the heroin entering the United States passed through a company named KINTEX which was run by the Bulgarian secret service, the Reagan administration disclosed.

June 27: In a rare public appearance before the Senate Judiciary Committee's subcommittee on the *Constitution* chaired by Sen. Orrin Hatch, R-Utah, the Rev. Sun Myung Moon asked Hatch to seek a Justice Department "prosecution memorandum" recommending that he not be indicted because the government had no case.

Rev. Moon said the memorandum, drafted during the Carter administration, was the unanimous opinion of three tax lawyers at the Justice Department whose job was to review cases for potential prosecution. Their recommendations were overruled twice by a "political appointee" with little experience in criminal tax cases, he said.

Rev. Moon said that in light of the hundreds of millions of dollars he had spent in the United States from foreign branches of the Unification Church, it was ludicrous to think he intended to cheat the IRS out of some $7,000 in taxes on a disputed sum of $25,000 over a period of 3 years.

According to earlier reports, Rev. Moon contended that the government's charges against him were racially motivated and were intended to attack the Unification Church, which he founded. "I would not be standing here today if my skin were white and my religion were Presbyterian," he told a crowd in Foley Square in New York following his indictment in October, 1981.

July 24: Democratic vice presidential nominee Geraldine Ferraro declined to comment on the alleged connection of her husband's real estate company to a Manhattan building described by police as an organized crime controlled distribution center of pornographic literature.

New York City records showed that the Zaccaro company, which was headed by Ferraro's husband John Zaccaro, paid the taxes on the seven-story building. A document on the building identified Zaccaro as the rental agent, as did the building's superintendent.

The building housed the distribution headquarters of Star Distributors, Media Distributors and Bonate Inc., all described by police as among the leading wholesale suppliers of hardcore pornographic magazines. Law enforcement sources said the companies were run by Robert DiBernardo, who directed distribution of pornography for the Gambino and DeCavalcante organized crime families.

Subsequent articles in the series, which won a national Investigative Reporters and Editors award, revealed other properties in lower Manhattan with mutual ties to organized crime figures and Zaccaro. Additionally, Zaccaro ultimately acknowledged that his firm owned the building at 200 Lafayette St., and Geraldine Ferraro was identified as his sole partner in the company.

Aug. 22: In a dramatic policy reversal, China's Communist Party was reported to be encouraging religious activity for the past 2 years. A document on the policy change had been drawn up by the secretariat of the party's Central Committee and sent to party committees nationwide. The move was seen as a pragmatic step toward creating national unity and improving international contacts.

Aug. 31: WASHINGTON — The White House decided, against the urging of the State Department and the CIA, to release a declassified version of a top-secret report on Soviet treaty violations. The *New York City Tribune* obtained materials used to brief senior government officials on the report, and published some of them verbatim.

Geraldine Ferraro: Unseemly connections.

Sept. 10: WASHINGTON — The Senate Intelligence Committee weighed a congressional request to reopen its 1980 investigation of Walter Mondale's top foreign policy adviser David L. Aaron. The committee denied the request despite charges that the investigation was obstructed by political tampering and unwillingness to air explosive, top-secret information,

New York City Tribune

The 1980s
A Decade of
Exclusives

according to intelligence sources. The 1980 investigation reportedly cleared Aaron, then deputy national security advisor to President Carter, of charges that he revealed information that led to the loss of a deep cover spy working in the Soviet Foreign Ministry.

Oct. 17: ATHENS — Greece's biggest selling daily newspaper, *Ethnos*, was officially charged with tapping the telephone of a Western correspondent who said the paper was a propaganda vehicle for the KGB. *Ethnos* reported that Poland's Solidarity movement was the work of the CIA, the Vatican and the Mafia. It referred to Afghan guerrillas as "paid murderers." The correspondent, Paul Anastasi, wrote a book alleging that *Ethnos* was established after high-ranking KGB officers visited Athens in 1981 and concluded arrangements with publisher George Bobolas.

Oct. 29: WASHINGTON — The U.S. Commerce Department authorized the sale of $81,000 worth of dynamite and high explosives to Bulgaria during the first half of 1984, according to its own statistics. The sale was not blocked by U.S. export controls despite the fact that the Bulgarian state trading agency that handled explosives sales, KINTEX, had been identified by U.S. officials as a major conduit of illicit arms and narcotics to terrorists. KINTEX supplied weapons and munitions to Palestinian terrorists and Nicaragua, according to U.S. officials.

1985

Jan. 10: The widespread famine in Ethiopia was the fruit of Marxism Leninism and only marginally the result of natural causes, a Rand Corporation expert on Africa said. "There are many causes of the famine in Ethiopia." Paul Henze said. "The least important is nature itself — drought."

Jan. 14: WASHINGTON — The Soviet Union delivered $350 million worth of military equipment to Cuba in the first half of 1984, nearly tripling the number of MiG-23 combat aircraft brought to Cuba since 1982 and bringing the total MiG force in that country to more than 200 warplanes, accord ing to a report by the Defense Intelligence Agency

Feb. 5: A special report revealed that the College for Human Services recruited dozens of students from men's shelters and methadone clinics as part of an effort to secure federal grants. The students were enrolled in programs that were supposed

*Ethiopian child:
Starved by ideology.*

to turn out gradu ates qualified to work at daycare centers and mental health care organizations.

Feb. 28: WASHINGTON — The Soviet military was said to hold a clear margin of superiority over that of the United States in 26 of 29 categories used to gauge military strength, according to Pentagon documents. The documents showed a Soviet 3-to-1 advantage in intercontinental ballistic missile warheads and a 7 to-1 advantage in

long-range intermediate nuclear force warheads.

March 11: North Korea had increasingly taken the Soviet line, according to Vasily Matuzoc, a former member of the Soviet mission to North Korea who escaped to the West after racing across the 38th Parallel to South Korea under a hail of machine gun bullets that killed four Korean soldiers and wounded one American. Matuzoc told the *New York City Tribune* that the North Korean

*Kim Il Sung:
Bothered his
neighbors.*

shift resulted from economic difficulties, fear of South Korean and Chinese modernization and international political isolation after their bombing attack on South Korean officials in Burma. "When Kim Il Sung, leader of North Korea, visited Moscow eight months ago, the Soviets and Koreans resolved their ideological differences," he said. "Korea had been spreading propaganda about its 'pure' form of communism,... and was advocating an independent path away from Moscow."

April 17: In his quest for political dominance in Latin America, Fidel Castro forged a coalition of neo-Nazi kingpins with militias and Marxist terrorists said R. Bruce McColm at Freedom House. This networking phenomena, which he called "narcoterrorism," is the "biggest security threat now," he said. The media had overlooked this coalition, he said. "It's a very strange alliance. Some Latin America producers are bona fide neo-Nazis [with] a strong rightwing nationalist ideology — but an anti-American ideology — which is the most important thing for the Cubans."

May 29: A 500-page report on 2,000 major incidents of internal unrest in the Soviet Union over a 3-decade period was delivered to the CIA and the Defense Department who commissioned it, the *New York City Tribune* learned. The report was prepared by Soviet emigras and covered the period 1953-84. Disaffection among non-Russian groups had been growing and had become "uncontrollable," the report said, while the relationship between disaffected members of Soviet society and officialdom had become one of "increased tolerance on both sides."

July 5: A series told the story of John Noble, who was arrested by the Soviets in eastern Germany in July, 1945, and spent 9 1/2 years in detention and slavery in Soviet Bloc prisons, including 5 years in a Siberian concentration camp. Noble was one of only 15 Americans ever to return out of an estimated 4,000 to 5,000 U.S. citizens and military personnel captured by the

Soviets as they "liberated" Germany in 1945. Noble believed that at least 200 of those Americans continued to be held by the Soviets.

July 19: Australia's decision to appoint a suspected Soviet agent as Consul and Trade Commissioner to Vancouver, Canada, had created a political furor. David Combe, a former national secretary of the ruling Australian Labor Party had been called a security risk by Laborite Prime Minister Bob Hawke in 1983 because of his frequent contacts with the Soviet KGB. After enormous political and media pressure, Hawke reversed his position and gave Combe the appointment.

Aug. 12: Leftist journalist Wilfred Burchett was on the payroll of several communist governments during most of his working life and collaborated directly in their disinformation efforts among Western newspapers, including *The New York Times*, according to documents released by the Australian Security Intelligence Organization.

Aug. 25: TOKYO — The Soviet Union was reportedly using a port in Nampo in North Korea since April as a refueling base for its smaller warships. On Aug. 13, three warships visited Wonsan on the eastern coast of North Korea as part of a celebration of the 40th anniversary of Korean liberation from Japanese rule. Japanese Defense Agency sources said North Korea might offer important military bases for the Soviets like Cam Ranh Bay in Vietnam.

1986

Jan. 22: TOKYO — Japan's largest opposition party, the Japan Socialist Party, unanimously adopted a new platform that dropped any reference to Marxism/Leninism. The JSP's apparent departure from Soviet-style "social ism" was aimed at preventing further loss of supporters, and gaining middle of the road voters to strengthen its political powerbase.

Jan. 23: PARIS — At a time partial withdrawal of the 35,000 Cuban troops in Africa was being discussed, the North Korean presence there of soldiers, advisors, technicians and

*Fidel Castro:
Narco-terrorist.*

diplomats was going unnoticed, according to an extensive study published here. The total number of North Koreans in at least 12 African nations was estimated at between 8,000 and 10,000.

Feb. 10: A series, "Porn Kings," detailed the presence of organized crime in all aspects of the pornography industry. According to law enforcement sources the symbiosis had grown from its roots in New York's Times Square to a complex national network.

Feb. 11: Terrorist groups would wither and die were it not for state sponsors, said a special report by the International Security Council. A working group at an ISC conference in Tel Aviv identified a "radical entente" of nations that provided direct and indirect support to terrorist organizations.

New York City Tribune

The 1980s A Decade of Exclusives

Those nations were identified as Libya, Syria, Iran, North Korea, and Cuba.

Feb. 12: The "Porn Kings" series identified Richard Basciano as the undisputed porn king of Times Square. Basciano ran the Show World Center on Eighth Avenue and 42nd St. His partner was Theodore Rothstein, operator of Star Distributors, which, as the *New York City Tribune* revealed in 1984, leased space from John Zacarro.

Feb. 20: Treaties signed between Malta and countries like Libya and North Korea had disturbed the United States and its NATO allies diplomatic sources said. A defense treaty concluded between Libya and Malta in November, 1984, gave Col. Moammar Qaddafi the option to intervene in case of undefined threats or acts of aggression against the island. North Korea also signed an agreement in July, 1982, which provided military assistance to Malta.

March 3: WASHINGTON — Secretary of Defense Casper Weinberger in a confidential memo told President Reagan the best response to Soviet arms control violations, which he detailed, was "to press for full funding for SDI in the Congress."

March 21: Although Soviet authorities claimed that Ukrainian sailor Mirosiev Medvid was alive and well, professional photographers and airbrush artists told the *New York City Tribune* that photographs of the Ukrainian sailor who tried twice to defect to the United States last October were forgeries. The photographs which appeared in Soviet publications revealed a stripping line indicating that his image was inserted into a picture of his family.

Theodore Rothstein: Porn king.

April 21: WASHINGTON — Pentagon officials said a huge new Soviet missile tested on April 2 was significantly larger than the SS-18 and was therefore almost certainly in violation of the SALT II treaty. The missile was described as a successor to the SS-18 and was identified as an SS-X-26.

May 9: Mayor Koch, responding to a report in the *New York City Tribune*, said the City would not grant a permit to next month's gay/lesbian parade unless organizers scrapped their plans to name portable toilets along the route after homosexual rights opponents, such as John Cardinal O'Connor. Calling the campaign "obscene," Koch also said it was "inappropriate" for a City correction official to use his office to help organize the campaign. The inspector general of the City Department of Corrections began investigating the official, an executive assistant to the Correction Department commissioner.

July 31: A special report examined Soviet emigre crime groups that had become increasingly active in New York City. Some 400 to 500 emigres were known to be involved in 12 groups. Most of the emigres had been involved in crime before they left the Soviet Union.

Oct. 13: A Pulitzer Prize-winning journalist for *The New York Times* deliberately ignored the 1932 forced famine in the Ukraine for "cheap

careerist reasons" said prominent British Sovietologist Robert Conquest. He called the famine in which seven million died, "Stalin's war against the peasants." *Times*' correspondent Walter Duranite knew the truth and distorted it in articles that categorically denied the existence of the famine, he said.

Nov. 10: A large phased-array radar at Krasnoyarsk was an important part of a missile defense system for eastern and central Soviet Union and as such constituted a violation of the Anti-Ballistic Missile Treaty, said a senior Defense Intelligence Agency officer.

1987

Jan. 13: A Radio Free Europe/Radio Liberty report stated that "Russian patriotic propaganda" then being used by the government in Moscow was making a case for great Russian ethnic superiority over non Russian nations and ethnic groups in the Soviet Union. The special report listed other indications of increasing Russian nationalism within the Communist Party.

Feb. 3: Gen. Vernon A. Walters, the U.S. ambassador to the United Nations, told the *New York City Tribune* in an interview that the United States would direct the United Nations' attention to human rights abuses in Cuba. He said he would present a "dossier of Cuban crimes against human rights" to an upcoming meeting of the U.N. Human Rights Commission in Geneva.

March 19: A Roman Catholic bishop said that distributing birth control devices in City schools would promote promiscuity and must be blocked before AIDS "puts an end

Ed Koch: Cans plan.

to us all." Bishop Edward Egan was appearing at a hearing before the City Council's education committee on a resolution to allow school-based clinics to dispense contraceptives to secondary school students. "Try decency, try chastity, try Western civilization," Egan told the panel, as a means of halting the mounting incidence of AIDS.

March 27: LONDON — Britain's Labor Party had within its ranks several "agents of influence" for the Soviet Union who strove to break up the NATO alliance and portrayed the United States as the main enemy to world peace, a former labor minister told a London court. Lord Chalfont, an independent peer in the House of Lords and chairman of the All Party Defense Group, said he could name members of the Parliament who fit that description. He made the claims in the High

Court as he gave evidence for *The Economist* magazine, which was being sued for libel by the Greek newspaper *Ethnos*. The libel suit was prompted when *The Economist* alleged that *Ethnos* had been launched with a $1.8 million subsidy from the Soviets.

July 24: National Security Council Director Frank Carlucci was said to be purging his staff of staunch supporters of President Reagan. The most recent dismissal was NSC staff counterespionage specialist David Major. Major was responsible for security in counterintelligence programs and won high praise from senior officials in the U.S. intelligence community who were interviewed.

Aug. 25: BUDAPEST, Hungary — The MEV Corporation

Bishop Edward Egan: "Try chastity."

that supplied the Soviet military with computer chips for weapons systems had employees who had worked for the West's leading computer firms. Furthermore, the firm was insured by a U.S. company, which reimbursed it for an estimated $2 million in damage when its plant burned down. A spokeswoman for the insurer in New York refused to comment.

Oct. 15: A newsstand operator who said he was a Christian told the *New York City Tribune* that distribution companies cut back deliveries of popular publications after he told them he no longer wanted to sell pornographic magazines. As a result, he lost more than $100 a month in net income he said.

Oct. 31: A Soviet expert, himself a Soviet emigre and a columnist for the *New York City Tribune*, introduced evidence that a KGB-hatched cabal installed Mikhail Gorbachev as party leader in 1985. For 5 years, research showed, the way was paved for Gorbachev's rise to power by a series of "coincidental" deaths and purges of rivals engineered by the KGB under Yuri Andropov's guidance.

Nov. 18: BERLIN, East Germany — An elderly couple living in a comfortable apartment near the Berlin Wall were the authors of the theory that the worldwide AIDS epidemic began when the virus leaked out of a U.S. Army laboratory during experiments on biological warfare. U.S. officials said the Soviet Union orchestrated the complex disinformation campaign and targetted countries where U.S. bases were located. The theory was cited on the *CBS Evening News* by anchorman Dan Rather and was carried in more than 225 newspaper articles and radio reports according to State Department statistics.

Dec. 9: WASHINGTON — Arms control specialist Frank Gaffney said the Soviets had broken out of the Anti-Ballistic Missile Treaty even while signing the INF Treaty. The developing network of 10 large phased array radars and broadly distributed engagement radars and the deployment of a large number of nuclear armed interceptor missiles were only consistent with the first stage of a nationwide defense against U.S.

New York City Tribune

strategic forces, he said.

Dec. 17: WASHINGTON — The INF Treaty signing was almost called off, an official said, because the first picture that the Soviets provided of the critical SS-20 missile system was a simple photocopy of an American photograph of the Soviet weapon. "The only picture that we really wanted was a high quality color glossy of the SS-20 out of its cannister. The Soviets finally provided a grainy black and white photo although they had provided good quality glossy photos of other weapons systems under discussion," he said.

1988

Feb. 21: WASHINGTON — An array of former Reagan administration officials told the Senate Foreign Relations Committee that the Intermediate Nuclear Forces (INF) Treaty should not be ratified. Eugene Rostow, President Reagan's first Arms Control and Disarmament Agency director, said the INF treaty would encourage mutualism and accomodation toward the Soviets in Europe and Japan, or else ultranationalism and militarism. William R. Van Cleave, head of the Defense Group in President-elect Reagan's transition team, said, "The Soviets will have ample opportunity to supplant eliminated systems with other systems ... Or they may retain a covert SS-20 force should they wish to do so." Van Cleave also noted that the treaty left the SS-25, a variant of the SS-20, unconstrained.

March 30: Sexual scenes involving children were commonplace in the three most widely read men's pornographic magazines — *Playboy, Penthouse,* and *Hustler* — according to a study sponsored by the Justice Department. The three magazines, which together reach an estimated 25 percent of all male professionals and 27 million people per issue, were found to contain sexually oriented photographs or cartoons involving children on the average of nine times per issue, the researchers said.

March 30: The chairman of the Pulitzer Prize board this year was Roger Wilkins, a senior fellow at the Institute for Policy Studies (IPS), which is considered a leftwing think tank in Washington, D.C.

June 10: The CIA was reportedly preparing to hire the ultraliberal former staff director for the late Sen. Frank Church's Senate Intelligence Committee, said U.S. officials. They expressed shock at the CIA's efforts to hire William G. Miller as a consultant. Miller, once an anti war activist directed the Church committee during the heyday of Congress's anti-intelligence crusade of the mid-1970s.

June 10: After two days of silence, CBS denied the charge that cartoon superhero Mighty Mouse sniffed cocaine on a Saturday morning cartoon show. CBS and the cartoon's creator, Ralph Bakshi, said the powder was clearly "crushed flowers." Bakshi was best known for the X rated *Fritz the Cat* cartoon of the 1970s.

June 20: In an unprecedented event a group of Soviet officials engaged in a firey debate with a panel of Soviet emigres in New York, under the sponsorship of the *New York City Tribune.*

June 28: Barbara Walters was accused of dealing gently with Jane Fonda in their interview on ABC TV's *20/20* because the broadcaster's husband heads the company that marketed the actress's lucrative workout videos. Walters is

The 1980s
A Decade of
Exclusives

married to Merv Adelson, chief executive officer of Lorimar Tele Pictures Inc. The Fonda exercise videos had grossed more than $250 million. During the interview on June 17, Fonda apologized to veterans for her statements and actions during the Vietnam War, referring to them as "thoughtless and cruel."

July 18: A church founded sex education curriculum entitled "About Your Sexuality" aroused a storm of controversy among parents and clergy who said it contained outright pornography and encouraged sexual permissiveness and experimentation. Published by the Unitarian-Universalist Association and designed for children as young as 12, the film strips and films showed graphic color pictures of male actors engaging in anal intercourse and oral sex as well as most other forms of sexual intercourse.

September: An eight part series, "In Search of a U.S. Foreign Policy," featured interviews with the foreign policy advisers of presidential candidates George Bush and Michael Dukakis in an effort to identify their position on the need for a

more sharply focused U.S. foreign policy.

The series also examined two articles that proposed tenets of such a comprehensive strategy. One was the International Security Council's "Affirmative Strategy for the Free World." ISC president, Dr. Joseph Churba, in describing the 'affirmative strategy,' said that the "containment strategy which has been the centerpiece of U.S. policy toward the Soviet Union in the post-World War II era has reached its outer limits and a new approach is needed to respond to *glasnost, perestroika* and the arms control strategies of the Soviet Union."

Jane Fonda
Why Barbara went easy on her.

Oct. 28: An agreement between Spain and Cuba to establish an intelligence sharing liaison had generated deep concern among the U.S. intelligence community, sources said. If the liaison was concluded it would be the first time that a NATO country established intelligence ties to a Soviet Bloc country.

Nov. 3: Health Commissioner Stephen Joseph reversed his decision to locate a controversial needle exchange program in four sites throughout the City. Neighborhood residents and City officials had been up in arms about one of the sites since the *New York City Tribune* reported the previous week that the proposed center was only 50 feet from P.S. 33 in Chelsea.

Nov. 17: What appeared to be a major sabotage operation of the Cuban telephone system in Havana indicated a rising level of unrest in Cuba said reliable sources. All telephone, telex and facsimile transmission facilities were interrupted by a major fire that destroyed the third floor of the building in Havana that housed Cuba's main overseas telephone switching and transmitting center.

1989

Jan. 15: WASHINGTON — Vice President-elect Daniel Quayle's newly appointed national security advisor, Dr. Carnes Lord, said that the State Department was a menace to United States security and should be thoroughly reorganized so that the president, not assistant secretaries of state, more directly controls the making of U.S. foreign policy in an article that appeared in *Global Affairs* before his appointment.

Jan. 23: Peter Klebnikov, the *New York City Tribune*'s East Europe correspondent was expelled from Romania by officials of the Securitate, the secret police, on Jan. 21. Klebnikov had attempted to interview a dissident clergyman and to report on the planned destruction of Romanian villages by Communist Party leader Nicolae Ceausescu.

Olof Palme:
What the KGB knew and when.

Feb. 6: JERUSALEM — Prime Minister Yitzhak Shamir said the intifada riots were running out of steam in late 1988 before the surprise U.S. decision to talk with the Palestine Liberation Organization. The American decision gave great encouragement to leaders of the uprising he told a group of visiting foreign policy experts.

Aug. 14: A feminist group that supported abortion rights received support from media companies such as Capital Cities/ABC, Time Inc., and Home Box Office (HBO). These companies were thanked for their "very significant contributions" to the National Women's Political Caucus in a brochure distributed at its national conference.

Aug. 27: STOCKHOLM, Sweden — Members of the Swedish Secret Police (SAEPO) said the Soviet KGB had clear foreknowledge of the assassination of Swedish Prime Minister Olof Palme on Feb. 28, 1986. The mass media here were agog with the news that SAEPO members admitted to having bugged a Soviet diplomat and suspected KGB officer from 1985 to 1987. The press controversy here centered on the legality of the bugging, avoiding the question of whether the Soviets had a hand in murdering the country's leader.

Aug. 29: MOSCOW — A KGB press officer told the *New York City Tribune* that the policies of *glasnost* and *perestroika*, usually ascribed in the West to Mikhail Gorbachev, were in fact devised by former KGB chief and Communist Party Secretary Yuri Andropov.

CHAPTER 6

DONALD TRUMP IN SEARCH OF ANSWERS

~1985

When Donald J Trump appeared on the U.S. political landscape in 2015, I was an editor at the Washington Examiner.

Sun Myung Moon had died some three years earlier on Sept. 3, 2012, and I had left The Washington Times a few weeks later on Jan. 4, 2013, for a position as Associate Editor at Newsmax Media. Chris Ruddy was gearing up for Cable TV and there was a high turnover rate of editorial personnel. I helped with recruiting and the expansion of the Washington Bureau but then it was time to move on.

In 2015, I created and edited the daily Examiner Today e-letter under the direction of Editor Hugo Gurdon for a million readers outside the Washington, DC metropolitan area. At earlier, one-on-one meetings with senior Washington Examiner officials, I had proposed the edition for those Americans who thought differently than most Washingtonians and were more attuned to what I assumed were core Examiner editorial values.

From reader response, it was clear that Trump was far and away the most exciting story of the year for that generally conservative national readership. As the holidays approached, and I was preparing to move to a fulltime staff position, something else became clear. The management of the Washington Examiner did not share our readers' enthusiasm for the Trump phenomenon.

My days at the Examiner and two and a half decades in Washington journalism were coming to an end.

Going through boxes of records and memorabilia in preparation for selling our home in Northern Virginia, I came across a photo of a youthful Donald Trump with me at the East Side Conservative Club in New York City in about 1985 when I was Editor in Chief at the New York City Tribune. Trump had always allowed the club to use a room at the Plaza Hotel which he then owned. And he would show up at the annual dinners with Club President Tom Bolan and Bolan's law partner, the notorious and feared Roy Cohn.

[Trump later remarked, once he was in the White House, that he missed having an attorney like Cohn. That reminded me of my one experience with Cohn in which I was seeking a solution to an issue faced by the New York City Tribune. Cohn did not ask for a retainer or warn me about fees incurred. He simply picked up the phone and made a brief call. Problem solved. The boilerplate at the foot of the home page of WorldTribune.com, which I founded in late 1998, has always included the following:

- LEGAL COUNSEL: ROY M. COHN (1927-1986) BACKUP PARALEGALS: HAMMER, RUDE, HUSSEIN, NASTY AND TONG.]

As this is written, I have never had the opportunity to sit down and talk with President Trump as Chris Ruddy of

Newsmax often has. But I have always heard that Trump, like all good journalists, is constantly asking questions of those he meets.

One former Unification Church member whom I met for coffee in 2019 recalled meeting the business tycoon and future president while fundraising in Connecticut in the late 1970s or early '80s. Trump told her that his staff took care of money while he was in motion, but he asked whom she represented. She told him.

"Oh, Rev. Moon!" he exclaimed. "I would love to carry his briefcase for a day."

I was struck by this comment from an anecdote that

Donald J. Trump and the author (then New York Tribune Editor in Chief) at an East Side Conservative Club dinner at the Plaza Hotel. / Robert Morton

occurred during the height of persecution against Sun Myung Moon and his followers.

How many other prominent Americans, including journalists, in those days of non-stop negative publicity would have felt that they could learn something from an oriental messiah by not only listening to him but serving as his temporary assistant?

That encounter provided a significant insight into the character of a man who would later be the 45th president of the United States. In my opinion, Donald Trump serves as an example to all Americans with his work ethic that includes continuously learning in order to make the best deals and decisions regardless of conventional wisdom.

That brings me back to the role of the American Free Press which is to provide the most authoritative information available to the people who must choose and guide the leaders of their government. To do so, working journalists must be open-minded, constantly curious and both willing and determined to question authority, whether government officials or the presumptions of peers and supervising editors and publishers.

It was Donald J Trump who famously and repeatedly called out and countered the "Fake News" that facilitated the corruption of American politics and culture in the 20th and early 21st centuries. There was another man who shared that passion for press freedom and freewheeling competition in the marketplace of ideas — the native North Korean, Sun Myung Moon.

CHAPTER 7

THE IRS OFFICE AT UNIFICATION CHURCH HEADQUARTERS

1978

It should never come as a surprise when the Internal Revenue Service of the U.S. government's Department of the Treasury launches an investigation of a conservative public figure or organization. But the targeting of Sun Myung Moon and my unlikely involvement as a reporter covering that investigation raises questions not easily answered.

It's a significant story, only part of which is recorded here, but first let's set the stage.

1970s: Revolution from the Far East

The world has changed dramatically since the turbulent years in the United States following its defeat in the Vietnam War and the Watergate scandal that drove a conservative president from the White House.

The name Sun Myung Moon has faded from public consciousness in the new millennium, and is rarely mentioned even by his own wife, Hak Ja Han, or the tens of thousands of couples he matched and blessed in marriage.

However, in the 1970s, that name had become a household

word in the United States, and that was intentional, Sun Myung Moon said.

He told his followers that God wanted to bring a revolution of heart in the United States. He succeeded in this goal not through slick, provocative PR or promotional campaigns but by bringing results and as he always did, by fearlessly confronting conventional wisdom and the "norms" of society at odds with the message he was obliged to deliver.

Those results included thousands of young people who shed their long hair and beards, donated their belongings to the "movement" and emerged as fresh-faced, patriotic, neatly dressed Americans following a Korean messiah they called "True Father". Speaking tours by "Rev. Moon" were organized in all 50 states, culminating in mass rallies in Yankee Stadium and at the Washington Monument in 1976.

Some of their parents from the "Greatest Generation", initially pleased by the change in appearance of their wayward sons and daughters, became alarmed by sensational media reports and came to see the "yellow peril" at work. After all there was nothing "normal" about the lifestyle of Unification Church members who got little sleep and took part in fundraising and mission work far from home. Many parents fought back, hiring deprogrammers to return their children to "normalcy" with all that entailed even if it meant free sex, drugs and rock and roll.

Established Jewish and Christian organizations mounted well-funded campaigns that lobbied the U.S. government to take action against an anti-communist (read fascist) oriental menace depicted as a pied piper leading young Americans astray. Sen. Robert Dole, an establishment Republican called for hearings which established Sun Myung Moon as a social-political issue in need of a reckoning.

But the most serious political agitation against this new foreign splinter in the American body politic came from the Left. Democrat Congressman Donald Fraser launched aggressive investigations and demanded action. Leftist news accounts depicted Sun Myung Moon as a sinister anti-communist religious charlatan, combining Christianity and Far East mysticism.

All of this made for a provocative media narrative that snowballed with very little in-depth reporting and fact-checking and almost no effective push-back from a new Christian religion from the Far East.

While Christian missionaries had spread the faith to the Orient, the reverse was now happening. A messianic movement from Korea and Japan was putting down roots in an unwelcoming culture, the USA.

By the 1970s, U.S. media had become a leftist force inclined to the Marxist view of religion as the "opiate of the masses." But in the interests of maintaining its all-important credibility and commercial traction in the marketplace of ideas (finally fully abandoned in 2016 with the election of President Donald Trump), the focus was on meeting its audience halfway. In other words, media professionals still officially upheld traditional standards of American journalism and sought the appearance of objectivity.

It's important to understand how journalism worked in practice in those days before Donald J. Trump. Reporters started an assignment by reviewing published articles that provided the context and record on which to build an updated, localized report. Working on deadline, they were typically not inclined to second-guess that context but merely to "top" it with new developments and quotes. Certainly, Sun Myung Moon was not available for interviews, and a two-day seminar on his teachings would have been required for any reporter seriously interested in understanding the phenomenon they were covering.

Sun Myung Moon as a threat to political establishments was nothing new and not a phenomenon that started in the United States. He had done prison time multiple times in both North and South Korea and in Japan, and not for any specific crimes committed.

He had been regarded as a political threat made more sinister and mysterious by the fact that he did not operate as a militant radical or politician but as a spiritual teacher who transformed the lives of those who followed his teachings. He was dangerous and a disruptor of society and state-recognized churches, especially in the newly communist nation of his birth, North Korea that had started cracking down on all churches. In 1947 he was convicted without evidence of spying for South Korea and given a five-year sentence to the notorious Hungnam labor camp. The inmates at Hungnam regularly dropped dead from long-hours of back-breaking labor and starvation. The invading UN forces lead by Gen. Douglas MacArthur bombed the camp resulting in the release of Sun Myung Moon in 1950, days after the onset of the Korean War and shortly before he was scheduled to be executed.

From one point of view, to be an anti-communist in the 1970s or an outspoken conservative in the '80s, '90s' and the new millennium should be as American as apple pie, but the opposite is true. Such views make one a lightning rod for attack from an anti-conservative establishment that bows to the Left. There are countless examples of the demonization of polarizing political figures like Ronald Reagan and media leaders like Rush Limbaugh.

By 1978, the political pushback against the anti-communist spiritual teacher who had already launched a New York City daily newspaper and would later establish The Washington Times took a familiar turn. The IRS was deployed.

The IRS Investigation

On the morning of Feb. 1, 1978, I got a news tip I will never forget.

Only 13 months earlier, I had been the acting managing editor of the New York News World daily at its startup on Dec. 31, 1976. Then I had returned to Austin in the summer of 1977 to write the thesis[1] for my master's degree in Journalism from the College of Communications at the University of Texas. Upon my return to the City that autumn, I had been selected as the newspaper's first foreign correspondent, based in Tokyo where Sun Myung Moon's first newspaper, Sekai Nippo, had started up in 1974. Due to bureaucratic delays in securing my journalist visa, I was on that morning working as a general assignment reporter who sometimes drafted "Editor's Journal" columns for the Editor.

---

1 "The Making of a New Metropolitan Daily in New York: The News World," published in the book "The News World of New York City: A Retrospective," 2023, Origin 2021 Publishing.

An authoritative source assured me that IRS agents were operating out of an office at the Unification Church national headquarters on 43rd St. in Manhattan. The implication was that a secret and hostile audit was being conducted with a complicit target. What's more, neither the public nor rank-and-file Unification Church members were aware of that investigation.

Our newsroom was located just a few blocks south at 401 Fifth Ave. One other reporter had already checked out the tip by contacting the American president of the Unification Church, Neil Salonen. For whatever the reason, he had dropped the story. I opted for the direct approach. Contacting a News World photographer, Michael Lograsso, I asked him to join me for a stroll up to 43rd St. with his cameras and that I would explain later. At the church headquarters, we entered, and I struck up a conversation with a building security guard. "Hey, what's this I hear about IRS agents operating on site?"

"Oh yeah," he responded. "They're working in the storefront office." He offered to take me there. It was one door East of the main entrance at 4 West 43rd St.

Out on the sidewalk, I instructed Lograsso to start taking pictures the moment we entered the office. I walked in and introduced myself as a reporter for the New York News World. There were two older men wearing glasses, one tall and balding, the other wiry and bearded working at desks. A young man, later confirmed to be a Unification Church member, appeared to be assisting them with files and documents. I asked what they were working on and if they were employed by the Internal Revenue Service.

Panic ensued as flashes from Mike's camera illuminated the scene. The two IRS agents quickly moved outside on the sidewalk, and one placed a call at the pay phone. Within moments, the tall figure of Unification Church Treasurer Keith Cooperrider, later an executive at The Washington Times, emerged from the main entrance and approached us. I introduced myself as a reporter and asked what was going on in the store-front office. No comment.

Upon returning to the office, I placed calls to the IRS and to Unification Church Headquarters, both of which brought threats of legal action against me and the New York News World if any article disclosing the investigation we had just exposed were published. The following article and photos appeared the very next day, Feb. 2, 1978:

IRS secretly involved in long-term scrutiny of Unification Church

By Robert Morton
News World Staff

It's that time of the year when income taxes are on everyone's mind — from tax collectors to taxpayers, presidents to paupers.

But the U.S. branch of the Unification Church, founded by the controversial Rev. Sun Myung Moon of South Korea, has been under close scrutiny by the Internal Revenue Service for nearly two years, according to informed sources. And a spokesman for the Church said that two IRS auditors had been working in an office of the Church's national headquarters on 43rd Street for almost one year on a daily basis.

Caught in the act

Yesterday, two investigators were discovered poring over the Church's books in a comfortable office which opens directly onto 43rd Street and is adjacent to the main entrance of the headquarters building.

They refused to divulge what they were doing, however, or how long they had been working there or what their names were even though they requested and were allowed to examine the reporters' press credentials. At this point the confusion snowballed.

Immediately after the reporters departed, the two men ran to the public pay phones on the sidewalk directly outside the office and placed a call.

Public relations officials for both the Unification Church and the IRS later acknowledged talking to the men, one of whom was referred to as Mr. Raymond, the same afternoon.

Are they or aren't they?

Milton Waldman, a spokesman for the district IRS office at 120 Church St., said he "could neither confirm nor deny" that IRS employees were auditing the Church's books. But he did say — in an apparent contradiction — that the two IRS employees at the Church had requested their photographs not be printed in The News World.

Even though he could neither confirm nor deny the presence of the two agents, Waldman warned that a

$5,000 fine and/or a five-year sentence could be slapped on The News World if it printed photos of the IRS agents.

A spokesman for the Unification Church said, "The Church officially has no comments on this matter." However the spokesman earlier quoted employee Raymond as warning that if anything was printed about him in the paper, the IRS would sue the Church.

Waldman said, "We are mandated to audit all exempt organizations" periodically according to a recently passed law. He refused, however, to name other churches similarly under audit. He did say that he was not aware of more people being hired by IRS to handle the additional workload. "The government has not been that generous with us," he explained.

Clearly the prolonged scrutiny of the Unification Church's exempt status would indicate that it is high on a priority list of organizations to be investigated. But Waldman would not comment on whether such a list existed or whether any wrong doings had been discovered.

He also refused to comment on how the investigation of the Church was prompted, although he said orders for audits come from the Department of Exempt Organizations and Employees Plan at the national IRS office in Washington, D.C., or the regional office in New York City. But "the regional office," he added, "will not talk to you."

While Unification Church officials were clearly surprised and irate at The News World's discovery of the

IRS accountants yesterday, some of them have privately expressed irritation at the prolonged investigation and have tried to avoid further pressure by seeking to avoid all publicity about the case.

Some observers, both members and non-members of the Church, have charged the IRS with discrimination because of an over-long scrutiny of the Church accounts without drawing any formal conclusions. Because of the IRS policy of not commenting on investigations in progress, they have not sought to silence this kind of criticism, or to answer the numerous questions about the procedures.

The publication of the above article had in immediate impact on my relationship with the Unification Church, which had been at arms-length and became more so. A member of the 43rd St. church headquarters staff confided to me that a meeting had been convened following publication of the article at which the following was said: "If Robert Morton is ever be seen in this building again, he should be treated as if he is a reporter for the New York Times."

As this was written 44 years later, I have yet to hear an explanation for the Unification Church agreeing to provide the IRS an office in its national headquarters. What did Sun Myung Moon think of the article? Informed sources told me he was "ecstatic."

I choose to file this one under "Unsolved Mysteries".

IRS secretly involved in long-term scrutiny of Unification Church

P3A
2/2/79

By Robert Morton
NEWS WORLD STAFF

It's that time of the year when income taxes are on everyone's mind—from tax collectors to taxpayers, presidents to paupers.

But the U.S. branch of the Unification Church, founded by the controversial Rev. Sun Myung Moon of South Korea, has been under close scrutiny by the Internal Revenue Service for nearly two years, according to informed sources. And a spokesman for the Church said that two IRS auditors had been working in an office at the Church's national headquarters on 43rd Street for almost one year on a daily basis.

Caught in the act

Yesterday, two investigators were discovered poring over the Church's books in a comfortable office which opens directly onto 43rd Street and is adjacent to the main entrance of the headquarters building.

They refused to divulge what they were doing, however, or how long they had been working there or what their names were even though they requested and were allowed to examine the reporters' press credentials. At that point the confusion snowballed.

Immediately after the reporters departed, the two men ran to the public pay phones on the sidewalk directly outside the office and placed a call.

Public relations officials for both the Unification Church and the IRS later acknowledged talking to the men, one of whom was referred to as Mr. Raymond, the same afternoon.

Are they or aren't they?

Milton Waldman, a spokesman for the district IRS office, at 120 Church St., said he "could neither confirm nor deny" that IRS employees were auditing the Church's books. But he did say—in an apparent contradiction—that the two IRS employees at the Church had requested their photographs not be printed in The News World.

Even though he could neither confirm nor deny the presence of the agents, Waldman warned that a $5,000 fine and/or a five-year sentence could be slapped on The News World if it printed photos of the IRS agents.

A spokesman for the Unification Church said, "The Church officially has no comments on this matter." However, the spokesman earlier quoted employee Raymond as warning that if anything was printed about him in the paper, the IRS would sue the Church.

Waldman said, "We are mandated to audit all exempt organizations" periodically according to a recently passed law. He refused, however, to name other churches similarly under audit. He did say that he was not aware of more people being hired by IRS to handle the additional workload. "The government has not been that generous with us," he explained.

Clearly the prolonged scrutiny of the Unification Church's exempt status would indicate that it is high on a priority list of organizations to be investigated. But Waldman would not comment on whether such a list existed or whether any wrong doings had been discovered.

He also refused to comment on how the investigation of the Church was prompted, although he said orders for audits come from the Department of Exempt Organizations and Employee Plan at the national IRS office in Washington, D.C., or the regional office in New York City. But "the regional office," he added, "will not talk to you."

While Unification Church officials were clearly surprised and irate at The News World's discovery of the IRS accountants yesterday, some of them have privately expressed irritation at the prolonged investigation and have tried to avoid further pressure by seeking to avoid all publicity about the case.

Some observers, both members and non-members of the Church, have charged the IRS with discrimination because of an over-long scrutiny of Church accounts without drawing any formal conclusions. Because of the IRS policy of not commenting on investigations in progress, they have not sought to silence this kind of criticism, or to answer the numerous questions about its procedures.

CAUGHT IN THE ACT . . . were these accountants for the Internal Revenue Service (above) at the Unification Church's national headquarters on West 43rd Street. After declining to answer questions about what they were doing, they rushed to a pay telephone outside the office, apparently to call their superiors (below).

CHAPTER 8

THE FAR EAST AND OTHER THINGS MY WIFE AND I HAVE IN COMMON

As "participant-observers" our story is relevant,
if not central to this volume.

1980s

The Far East and a beautiful, spirited young woman who had never set foot in my homeland were unfathomable mysteries that proved irresistible to a lone wolf American newshound.

Journalists are a curious lot, and I had long been fascinated by the world outside the continental U.S., Northeast Asia in particular.

Before we met for the first time, in Europe in 1981, South Korean native Shin Choon Boon translated in Germany for a Korean man, Sung-San Lee, organizing seminars on journalism for a news service called Free Press International.

Lee was a former translator for U.S. Army Intelligence in South Korea who joined Sun Myung Moon's Unification Church and was later dispatched to New York City to explain to the management and staff of the New York News

World what communism means, in reality as opposed to theory. In short order, he became the temporary owner's representative at the company, and fireworks ensued back in New York City.

Half a world away, as the Tokyo correspondent for The New York newspaper, I was blissfully unaware of any of these developments. Meanwhile, Miss Shin was working as a skilled operating room RN in Frankfurt, West Germany. She was also far from her birthplace. Neither of us knew the other existed.

My paychecks were issued by News World Communications, Inc., the parent company of the New York newspaper and later of The Washington Times. One summer day in 1978, I noticed that the name on the paycheck had changed to Free Press International. That was the first time I ever heard of the news service that was now paying our New York daily's foreign correspondents.

I would meet Miss Shin in Europe about three years later, after I had returned to New York. Subsequently I was promoted to editor in chief of the newspaper and assigned responsibility for Free Press International (FPI). On a trip to Turkey, Germany and UK to explore new media ventures for FPI, Miss Shin and I met for the first time in Frankfurt, a story in and of itself.

Back in New York, my staff test-marketed a mailed weekly Free Press International News Service package and published a successful bi-weekly newsletter, the FPI International Report, that was modeled after the Economist's Foreign Report.

The owner's representatives at the company asked me to

Miss Shin in Frankfurt in 1977.

report about these new media ventures. The Founder seemed pleased with my update. When I explained the concept for FPI International Report (national and foreign correspondents often have access to intelligence information not suited for general interest newspaper reports but relevant for subscribers to a geostrategic newsletter), Sun Myung Moon seemed intrigued and requested that his oldest son Hyo Jin receive a subscription.

Between 1980 and 1991, FPI International Report did well and operated in cooperation with the International Security Council (ISC), a policy institute also founded by Sun Myung Moon and directed by Dr. Joseph Churba, a Syrian Jew born in Brooklyn who was former U.S. Air Force Middle East Intelligence estimator and a key national security advisor to Ronald Reagan in the 1980 campaign.[1] I had met and interviewed him in 1980 and in the following years strategized with him about the formation and naming of the ISC. The late journalist Sol Sanders and I served as senior editors of the ISC's quarterly journal, Global Affairs.

The Founder subsequently spoke often of an international news network. (His key assistant, Col. Bo Hi Pak, who in 1981 became president of all U.S. media projects, prioritized an emphasis his team considered more practical: a lone Washington-based newspaper to deliver political impact nationally and internationally from the capital of the Free World.)

The latter vision prevailed, and FPI suspended publication, along with the New York City Tribune on Jan. 4, 1991. [See Chapter 11, The Unnatural 'Suspension' of the NYC Tribune]. The International Security Council suspended operations a few years later.

The Far East and Gen. Shin's Descendant

Miss Shin was born in Namhae, South Korea into a large

---

1   From the New York Times obituary of April 28, 1996: "Joseph Churba, who was the Air Force's top Middle East intelligence expert in 1976 when he publicly criticized comments by the Chairman of the Joint Chiefs of Staff, Gen. George S. Brown, about Israel's being a military burden for the United States, died on April 18 at Lenox Hill Hospital. He was 62 and moved to midtown Manhattan from Washington in January.

— The cause was a heart attack and he had pancreatitis, said Sol W. Sanders, a friend.

— At his death Mr. Churba was president of the International Security Council, a Washington-based research institute. He was a Presidential campaign adviser to Ronald W. Reagan in 1980 and an adviser to the Arms Control and Disarmament Agency in 1981 and 1982.

— Mr. Churba made his unusually blunt criticism of the top service officer in telephone conversations with a reporter on Oct. 19, 1976. Mr. Churba said that General Brown's comments had been "dangerously irresponsible" because they encouraged the Arabs and Russians to think American backing for Israel had diminished. He said the comments were indicative of a growing "tilt against Israel in the Defense Department."

and exceptional family (that subsequently included medical doctors, professors, a Harvard graduate and a Seoul-based editor of a major newspaper). After the Korean War, her father moved his family to Busan where they thrived but not without sacrifice and heartaches. The family's strength and exceptionalism traces to their ancestral heritage.

Hundreds of years earlier, the legendary Gen. Shin Sung-Gyeom, their ancestor according to the Shin family records, sacrificed his life for his king, Wang Geon, (having dressed in the king's armor and allowing the king to escape) which preserved the Goryeo kingdom he had persuaded the king to establish. The modern name Korea is derived from Goryeo. Today there are shrines in Gen. Shin's honor throughout South Korea.

According to Wikipedia, supplemented by Korean references:

> The Pyeongsan Shin (平山申氏) clan is a Korean yangban (aristocratic) family, which takes its root during the 10th century Goryeo dynasty. At the beginning of the Goryeo period, the country was divided in several kingdoms fighting for supremacy over the Korean peninsula.
>
> The founder of the clan was Gen. Shin Sung-Gyeom, who helped King Wang Geon found the Goryeo Kingdom by dethroning the tyrant Gung Ye . . . in 918.
>
> As described on an official description plate at his memorial shrine in the province of Gangwon-do [northeast South Korea], Shin Sung-Gyeom was killed instead of the king [and decapitated, his head taken as a trophy] in 927 in a battle in modern-day Daegu, fighting bravely

The three grave sites of Gen. Shin Sung-Gyeom in Gangwon-do Province, above, and a statue, below, in a memorial park in his honor in Daegu city.

in the king's armor, riding his white horse to save King Wang Geon, who formally founded the Goryeo Kingdom in the same year. After his death, the King bestowed the high aristocratic title of JangJeolGong [장절공]… [Wang Geon loved Shin and honored his filial piety by ordering a head of pure gold to be buried with the body. To prevent grave robbery, he built 3 tombs although the body was in only one. Shin's body was found based on his birthmark on his left foot (moles in shape of the Big Dipper (북두칠성)].[2]

Fast forward to the twentieth century when the Korean nation was finally occupied by its enemy Japan in 1910 and then fought for and won back its independence in 1945 only to be split in two by the great powers following World War II. The Shin family, like many South Koreans lost much of what they owned during the occupation followed by the Korean War and had to start from scratch in the aftermath.

What struck my wife and me as a miraculous coincidence was how two people from contrasting backgrounds and opposite sides of the globe became separately involved with an obscure news service neither of us had ever heard of. Just as her life and work in Europe as a Registered Nurse with a gift for languages and later a writer herself prepared her to become an American citizen and my soul mate, my work in the Far East likewise readied me for her. It also opened my eyes to the dawn of the coming Pacific Century.

---

2 https://en.wikipedia.org/wiki/Pyeongsan_Shin_clan

Foreign Correspondent

Living and working in Tokyo from 1978-80 proved a fascinating life experience. I found the day-to-day discipline and adventure of reporting the news from one of the most foreign countries an American could imagine an exhilarating experience. In retrospect, it was the most fulfilling professional activity in a decades-long media career. Covering the news in Tokyo and Seoul shaped my attitudes about and enthusiasm for journalism and the American free press not to mention Northeast Asia.

Because my travels took me to South Korea, China, Taiwan, Southeast Asia and Hong Kong, I learned firsthand about the Asian mindset and culture. Those insights served me well when, back in the United States, I would work for two major metropolitan daily newspapers managed at the highest levels by Korean men. My years as foreign correspondent also served as insightful background, oddly, for life in Washington, D.C. where the People's Republic of China had bought influence on an extensive scale by the close of the 20th Century.

My first byline from Japan topped a first-hand report about the student riots at the Narita Airport then preparing to open, replacing the outgrown Haneda Airport closer to downtown on the Tokyo Bay. I interviewed the Red Army students living with the farmers they sought to radicalize in their bid to stop the march of U.S.-inspired "capitalist imperialism" which they hated. One young man reminded me of Unification Church members in the U.S. who in those years lived with the daily threat of being kidnapped and "deprogrammed" by thugs hired by their own parents because they were depicted in press reports as brainwashed dupes of a Korean messiah.

"My parents don't like what I am doing with my life," he said, "but some of my friends understand." That interview ran as a sidebar to my report from Narita about the Shinto

Expert says plant workers overreacted

By Robert Morton
NEWS WORLD FOREIGN STAFF

4-4-79

TOKYO—A top U.S. nuclear expert here said yesterday that technicians overreacted to mechanical failures at the Three Mile Island nuclear plant and unwittingly triggered last week's "incident."

The expert, who asked not to be identified, said that night-shift operators ████████ and ████ made two significant mistakes in their response to the crisis at the nuclear plant, although they were acting "in all good faith."

The source, a high-level official in the U.S. nuclear industry, said he based his conclusion on constant communications with the Nuclear Regulatory Commission (NRC), Metropolitan Edison and industrial sources.

[A person answering the telephone last night at the residence of ████████ in Middletown, Pa., hung up when a reporter identified himself asking for comment.

████████ reached last night by telephone at the residence of ████

(Continued on Page 4A)

PANIC

FROM PAGE 1A

████ also in Middletown, said that he did not wish to comment on any aspect of the accident. She also refused to reply to the charges, referring instead to utility officials. In Washington, D.C., a spokesman for the NRC declined to comment on the report of human failure.]

Panic

During the panic-filled five minutes between the initial pump failure and the first release of radioactive steam, the operators took unnecessary measures which led to the nation's worst nuclear accident in history, the source said.

"Without those two actions, there would have been no appreciable core ceremony with which the airport was finally dedicated in May 1978 after five years of delays and 12 years of demonstrations and violence. Crossing back and forth between to airport grounds and the demonstrators to conduct interviews, I was teargassed for my trouble and nearly got hit by a hurled Molotov cocktail.

In retrospect, 1978 during the final dark years of the Carter Administration, was a surreal time captured in my mind's eye by the imagery of that showdown in the rural countryside outside ultra-modern Tokyo between those young Japanese Red Army communists and police dressed in Darth Vader-like protective gear.

One exclusive from the Far East ironically zoomed in on breaking news back in the United States. Following sensational reports on the partial meltdown at the Three Mile Island nuclear reactor in Pennsylvania, I got a call from a source for an article I had written about American firms involved in building nuclear reactors in energy-starved Japan. This senior official for Westinghouse Nuclear in Tokyo had earlier sought my help in joining the prestigious Foreign Correspondent Club of Japan.

"Human error," he informed me about the crisis at Three Mile Island. Requesting anonymity, he offered access to a live fax feed from the Nuclear Regulatory Commission (NRC) and direct industry sources. My front-page story of April 4, 1979, carried the headline: 'Expert says plant workers overreacted'. The New York desk contacted the NRC and technicians named in my story. All declined comment.

Unlike most other western Tokyo correspondents who lived and socialized with non-Japanese, I roomed with the foreign editor of the Sekai Nippo, the first newspaper founded by Sun Myung Moon. The late Takefumi Miyagi had graduated from Tokyo University and as a serious journalist had become a close friend. He tolerated my endless questions and countless challenges as I sought to wrap my mind around the infinite cultural contradictions that Japanese group-oriented culture and tradition posed to all that I represented as an individual-istic American of Protestant Christian origins. I was fascinated by the pervasive samurai code of honor as well as the charm, femininity and strength of Japanese women in a society that was itself feminine but far from feminist.

My first trip to Seoul, South Korea broadened perceptions of two Asian cultures as strikingly different as cats and dogs.

The energy in the streets of Tokyo and Seoul offered a study in contrasts. Japanese faces masked human interactions operating on multiple levels of etiquette as challenging to foreigners as mastering the Kanji Chinese characters that interspersed the language. Koreans, on the other hand, were open books, and their interactions on the streets, like bumper cars at amusement parks, were less formal and more direct and emotional with hearts as hot as the cuisine.

Modern Japan had been transformed by Gen. Douglas MacArthur's post-World War II occupation but was cultur-ally still the preserve of Shinto and Buddhist priests. Korea, I came to realize had core Confucianist traditions with strong Buddhist influence. But in 1978, the national culture had passionately embraced Christianity.

It's fair to say that I admired the Korean tribe, with indi-vidual exceptions, and looked forward to assignments that took me to Seoul. I was home on leave and sitting in our

Washington Bureau at the National Press Club building when the Reuters wire brought the news on Oct. 26, 1979, that South Korean President Park Chung-Hee had been assassinated. I caught the very next flight out of Dulles on Northwest Airlines.

The fear in the streets of Seoul was palpable. A nation that remembered and was still recovering from the Korean War half-expected the North to take advantage of the riots in the South for democracy and the killing of its president by his intelligence chief and once again launch an invasion. A waitress in a downtown restaurant, who did not know me from Adam, proposed marriage. She made no bones about it: She wanted out.

Getting at the story of the assassination and the power struggle that ensued was not easy and included dropping in for briefings at the U.S. embassy and trading information with Korean journalists not free to report for their newspapers much of what they actually knew. Examples included the identity of late night passengers in cars arriving in parking lots at the Ministry of Defense. I managed to obtain a copy of the martial law government's official report on the Park Chung-Hee assassination from young Gen. Chun Doo-Hwan [later to become president]. I rushed back to the Grand Hyatt Hotel where my friend Kyung Soon Lee managed the Business Center and its telex machine operators in the days before laptops. My colleague Don Kirk was there as well and together we filed our reports back to New York. His to the NY Times and mine to The New York News World.

Ten years later, I had a surprise visitor at my Fifth Ave. New York City Tribune office in New York. Kyung Soon Lee had graduated from the Columbia University School of Journalism and was working as managing editor of the New York edition of Hankuk Ilbo, no mean feat for a Korean woman in the late 1980s.

One year later, as detailed elsewhere in this volume, the New York City Tribune suspended publication as did its news service, Free Press International.

In late 1991, my wife and I and our 4-year-old daughter Laurene, moved to Falls Church, Virginia, and I began a 21-year stint at The Washington Times which ended just weeks after the passing of Sun Myung Moon in 2012.

After working as Associate Editor at Newsmax and Examiner Today Editor at the Washington Examiner (2013-2015), I independently established Free Press Foundation (freepressfoundation.org) as a 501 (c)(3) in North Carolina in 2016. Two years later, with the encouragement and support of its Advisory Board[3] I launched a news service to combat the "Mainstream Media" monopolies that had sapped the American Free Press spirit which helped make this country great. The name of this news service? Free Press International.[4]

Looking back, marriage has been an adventure and the key to happiness for both of us. True Love matters, although it is also an ideal that seems always just beyond reach. My wife communicates more effectively in spoken English than I. She is my most effective editor and has quickly adapted to other foreign languages as well. But her native tongue is Korean.

---

3 http://freepressfoundation.org/advisory-board/
4 https://freepressinternational.org/

We have lived as restless nomads, unmoored by geographic or family roots that nonetheless each of us cherish. To be sure, we are soulmates. And we also share a dedication to truth with a capital T and not just facts, limited as they are by geographic, cultural and generational bubbles.

At the same time, coming from opposite sides of the globe with different languages and traditions, we are fundamentally united in love for our children who represent the future.

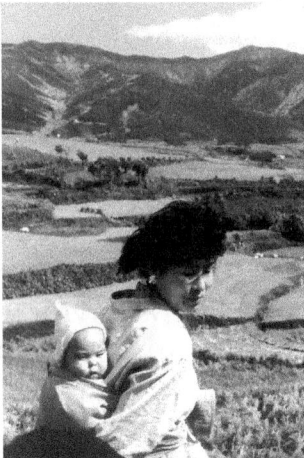

Laurene (with a makeshift cap and transportation on an unexpected windy day) with her Mother on a visit to a hillside in Namhae, South Korea in 1988. / Robert Morton

Laurene and her mother in Northern Virginia. / Robert Morton

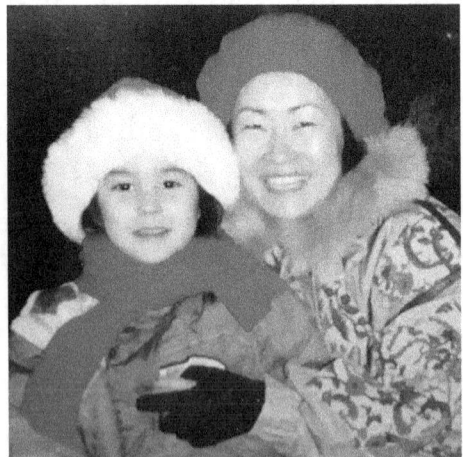

'God Bless the Child That's Got His Own'

Them that's got, shall get
Them that's not, shall lose
So the Bible said, and it still is news
Mama may have, and Papa may have
God bless' the child,
That's got his own
That's got his own
Yes the strong seem to get more

While the weak ones fade
Empty pockets don't
Ever make the grade
As Mama may have

And Papa may have
God bless' the child
That's got his own
That's got his own.

And when you got money,
You got a lots of friends
Crowdin' 'round your door
When the money's gone

And all you're spendin' ends
They won't be 'round any more
No, no, no more

Mama may have
And your papa may have

God bless' the child who can stand up and say
I've got my own
Ev'ry child's, got to have his own!

— Blood, Sweat & Tears

The highlight of the 1980s was the birth of our Laurene on a spring day in 1987 at the Lenox Hill Hospital in Manhattan.

April 28 began with a light but persistent rain as my wife's water broke. As the contractions increased, I went out for my company car parked on the streets of Sunnyside Queens. I could not spot it. Then there it was, sitting out in traffic. All four tires were flat and somehow it had been moved sideways out into the street. To this day I have no explanation. I called my friend, a few blocks away who had helped me move our baby furniture into our 4th floor walkup apartment, to borrow his brand new Sentra. His wife informed me he was on a train to Washington because their car had been stolen off the street the night before.

Unbelievable.

Adrenaline pumped as I began calling taxi companies that were all facing rain delays. Finally I found a company which, from the accents over the phone, I concluded was operated by foreigners. My sister in law, Mrs. Eu who had come from Korea to be with her next to youngest sister during child birth, helped me assist my wife down the stairs. She was in pain with back labor.

The driver, remarkably, was Korean and spoke little English. More to the point, he had no idea how to go to Manhattan, my wife murmured. As he urgently consulted his dispatcher on the radio, I used sign language to navigate him over the Queensboro bridge and then, turning right, up the East Side to Lenox Hill hospital. Dr. Pascario (who we later heard was also the baby doctor for model Jerry Hall, the futue Mrs. Rupert Murdoch) and his team of beaming nurses were waiting.

After that remarkable drama, the rest of the day was simply bliss as were the first cries of my daughter which came over the speaker into the waiting room. Holding her in my arms a few minutes later, I examined all her facial features, fingers and toes — Perfection, a miracle from Heaven above. My life to the core of my being had been changed forever by this beautiful princess and her dramatic entrance.

I am forever indebted to the NYC Tribune's Culture Editor, Patrick Martin, who came to the hospital, picked up my car keys, got that Honda Accord towed, repaired, and delivered back to the hospital.

Vivid in my memory are the waves of yellow spring daffodils on the median of Park Ave. as I drove home that evening, a proud new father. That morning I had experienced the wrath of Satan, followed by the infinite Love of God embracing our new family.

From New York City to the extremely multi-cultural Fairfax County in Virginia, Laurene grew with the serenity of that suddenly sunlit spring afternoon. Ballerina, honors student, fine arts graduate, art teacher to adoring children, photographer, happy wife, attentive and loving mother.

The Fairfax County schools of the 1990s featured extreme ethnic diversity with more than a hundred nationalities and multiple languages represented. So, race mattered not, or did it? As a sensitive Korean American, Laurene was keenly aware of her uniqueness. But she endured life's slights with silence and remarkable stoicism, not unlike her Grandmother Mary Hill Morton. And she was wise. Her friends in high school called her the judge.

Wanting no part of the political-media wars that had

marginalized her parents, Laurene transcended the Washington scene with grace and a 7-year hiatus in northern California where she and husband Dominick Lima welcomed another miracle, Adele Josephine, on Oct. 1, 2020. Then it was back to the reality East of the Mississippi River.

How was it that Laurene managed the powerful forces impacting her life, harmonizing them with a strong original mind and character that insisted on finding her unique path forward?

"....God bless' the child who can stand up and say I've got my own."

CHAPTER 9

MATT DRUDGE:
'LET THE FUTURE BEGIN'

1998

In late 1998, I launched WorldTribune.com.

Also in 1998, a young misfit named Matt Drudge rocked the political and journalistic establishment by publishing a story spiked by Newsweek Magazine on his makeshift html web site DrudgeReport.com. That article detailed one of Bill Clinton's sensational sex scandals in the White House.

DrudgeReport quickly became must-reading in Washington and soon eclipsed (in Internet readership) the major American dailies it frequently linked to.

A year earlier, as editor of The Washington Times National Weekly Edition, I had been invited as a Media Fellow to the Hoover Institution at Stanford University where I made a presentation on the State of the American Newspaper. In that talk, I noted that paid combined circulation of morning and afternoon newspapers nationwide had remained essentially flat, increasing by only a million during the period from 1954 after the Korean War to 1994, following Whitewater scandal, when the nation's population had grown by 130 million.[1]

---

1   See additional detailed data in Chapter 1, of the author's master's degree thesis at the University of Texas at Austin: "But at the same time urban concentration is increasing, the

Matt Drudge reading the Washington Times National Weekly Edition. / Robert Morton

Taking the research from those remarks as the writing on the wall, and concerned about the future of American newspapers, I decided to launch my own Internet newspaper

relative number of daily newspapers per city is decreasing." Austin (1977, Robert J Morton) and book: The News World of New York City, 2023, Origin 2021 Publishing).

publishing the reporting and commentary of far-flung colleagues in the news business and a Mideast news service run by Steve Rodan, a former Jerusalem correspondent for the NYC Tribune. Rodan had gone on to work for the Jerusalem Post, developed excellent regional sources and then decided to strike out on his own.

My inspiration for this new venture came from two media revolutionaries: Sun Myung Moon and Matt Drudge.

The former had in 1997 directed Washington Times President Dong Moon Joo to establish an international newspaper with local editions in each nation and that would be affiliated with The Washington Times.[2]

The latter had demonstrated what could be done at almost no cost with simple html code.

When a colleague at The Washington Times invited me to join him for lunch with Matt Drudge at the Capital Grille, on Friday, Feb. 25, 2000, I readily accepted.

18 months earlier, Drudge had rocked the Washington press corps with a landmark speech at the National Press Club on June 2, 1998, which is reprinted at the end of this chapter.

Six months before that speech which turned out to be prophetic, he had shaken the political and media landscape to the core with a headline that established DrudgeReport. com as the go-to news site in the Internet era: 'NEWSWEEK KILLS STORY ON WHITE HOUSE INTERN' about Monica Lewinski and then President Bill Clinton ("I did not sexual relations with that woman"[3]).

---

2   Given the enormous subsidies required to sustain operations of The Times, the direction was deemed unrealistic.

3   Television address by Bill Clinton on January 25, 1998.

July 4, 2002 10:20 p.m. Washington, D.C.

Matt Drudge: I admire your efforts to tell the news as it really is. Keep an eye on Motorola and IBM to go belly up in the fourth quarter this year. IBM has the same problems as Enron and WorldCom, and Motorola is out of the game with telecom and Communications.. lost to overseas competition... I base this on over twenty years in the industry and see the writing on the wall... so to speak...

R Morton: Have been away at my 'print job. Don't know how you Follow all the fronts.

America Online Instant Message

Over a spirited lunch in the restaurant on Pennsylvania Ave. that caters to powerbrokers on and around the Hill, we discussed both the news of the day and the news business. I offered to tip him off on Washington Times stories that were about to go to press. He was delighted.

I then asked him about a static link for WorldTribune.com on the DrudgeReport.

"I've got a better idea," he responded. Drudge asked me to tip him off on breaking news of interest in WorldTribune.com and he would link to them.

The result was a seven-year unofficial partnership, using the AOL instant messenger, that greatly boosted daily traffic to the Washington Times web site. Furthermore, WorldTribune stories got millions of page views which helped build awareness for a non-capitalized news operation that would otherwise have languished in obscurity.

Over the next two years, I would invite Drudge to my table at the White House Correspondents Dinner. He came with his trademark fedora and had a blast, even going up to the

R Morton: How's about I buy you dinner this weekend?
R Morton: Or brunch?
R Morton: For an update on changing media scene in DC

Matt Drudge: Here
Matt Drudge: When are you down here
Matt Drudge: Where are you staying

R Morton: Will be down Saturday
R Morton: If you will be there

Matt Drudge: OF COURSE
Matt Drudge: WHERE WILL YOU BE?

R Morton: I don't know yet suggestions in the vicinity

Matt Drudge: It's jammed down here

R Morton: Doesn't matter. I'll work out something will confirm up time and touch base have a 1.5 year old cell number for you

Matt Drudge: XXX-XXX-XXX
Matt Drudge: I'm between XXX and XXX

R Morton: OK that's the one I have that's the one I had mine is
R Morton: XXX-XXX-XXX

Matt Drudge: I have a zero plan other than radio Sunday night and my dad is coming down at 4 PM on Sunday

R Morton: Have a flight arriving at four 8:45 AM
R Morton: Will probably return the same day as I have a trip to Asia coming up

Matt Drudge: You coming for the art show

R Morton: No just to see a couple other colleagues hopefully

Matt Drudge: OK let me know bells will be on I have a car

R Morton: Great look forward to it will call when headed your direction

Matt Drudge: 76 here tomorrow

R Morton: Beautiful

head table to greet President George W Bush and the First Lady Laura.

Back at our table, he mentioned that his bestseller, "The Drudge Manifesto", was doing very well. But, he confided, "I am not doing DrudgeReport for the money. The day I start doing this for the money, I'm finished."

After that memorable White House Correspondents Dinner, WorldTribune.com was contacted by a young man by the name of Kevin Lucido. He had left a prominent conservative publishing firm in Washington and launched a new advertising venture called Intermarkets. He signed a contract with WorldTribune to provide networked advertising using DoubleClick. What he was especially interested in, I came to realize, was connecting with the DrudgeReport.

Not a single advertisement resulted from that arrangement, and WorldTribune.com had to fight to get out of the contract after its first year. But Intermarkets emerged as the exclusive advertising partner for DrudgeReport, until it went over to the "Dark Side" in the eyes of many former fans in mid-2019[4].

The next year, Matt Drudge again accepted my invitation for his second and final White House Correspondents Dinner. This time he stayed at the Mayflower Hotel where we met before the reception. He confided that there was now a major new dimension in his life as a media star: "Kevin is sending me a check [for a very large number] every month and I don't know what to do with the money."

---

4   Drudge mystery: The brand lives, but who runs it and where is Matt?, WorldTribune.com, October 25, 2019, [https://www.worldtribune.com/drudge-mystery-the-brand-lives-but-who-runs-it-and-where-is-matt/]

In those early years of the Internet news revolution, traditional newspaper newsrooms responded with confusion, defensiveness and outright hostility to the onrushing Internet revolution which first encroached on and then ended their exclusive sovereignty over American news consumers' perceptions of reality. On his first visit to The Washington Times, Drudge dropped by the office of Editor Wes Pruden. Afterwards, he came to my office looking like a student just returned from a summons to the principal's office. "He gave me a lecture," he said, unbowed but with astonishment.

How this 7-year unofficial partnership with Drudge ended is a story for later.

It followed by one year my last meeting with him at his home, then, in Miami, Florida. Later and at my final meeting with the late Andrew Breitbart (who assisted Drudge and attended subsequent White House Correspondents Dinners in his stead), I realized that that meeting may have been one of the last with a fellow journalist by the famous recluse.

He picked me up in his souped-up Mustang and drove to his island home. The only other occupants as far as I could tell were his cats. He had laptops or computers in most rooms, and he showed me the programs admirers had set up to help him discern which stories on Drudge Report were hot. Later I rode in his pickup to his condo in the Four Seasons Hotel from which he had sent me images by AOL's instant messenger. There were windows facing out to sea, North toward Palm Beach and into downtown Miami.

I warned him that changes were afoot at The Washington Times, that others might want to displace me as his contact and that the newspaper's editorial positioning might even change. Months later, Drudge would IM me that "I see what you were talking about."

Before he dropped me back at my rental car, we sat outside the hotel and talked about my upcoming trip to Japan to recruit a "China-watcher" for our subscription e-letter Geo-strategy-Direct.com. He characterized that conversation about China as "inspiring".

Following is the text of his remarkable and prescient speech at the National Press Club on June 2, 1998:

> "Applause for Matt Drudge in Washington at the Press Club": Now there's a scandal. It's the kind of thing I'd have a headline for.
>
> I'd like to thank the president of the Press Club, Doug Harbrecht — thank you very much — for extending the invitation to address you today; and to Kerry Gildae, the brave member of the Speakers Committee, for suggesting it. Thank you very much.
>
> You know, last time I was in town — and this is my hometown, Washington; I grew up here — I arrived to a headline in the local paper: "I was baby-sat by Matt Drudge — Exclusive!" It quoted one of my elementary-school chums, "Even at age 12, Drudge already liked to tell stories. He'd take all the kids down to a creek behind my house when it was dark and tell us those elaborate stories. We'd be terrified." Well, the only thing that has changed is my shoe size.

You know, and what a place, Washington, DC, to grow up in. I used to walk these streets as an aimless teen, young adult; walk by ABC News over on DeSales, daydream; stare up at the Washington Post newsroom over on 15th Street; look up longingly, knowing I'd never get in — didn't go to the right schools, never enjoyed any school, as a matter of fact, didn't come from a well-known family — nor was I even remotely connected to a public — a powerful publishing dynasty.

Burning I may have been, but I was sophisticated enough to know I would never be granted any access, obtain any credentials, get that meeting with Vernon Jordan, or work with Newsweek magazine. There wasn't a likelihood for upward mobility in my swing-shift position at 7-11. (That was my last job in Washington.)

So, in the famous words of another newsman, Horace Greeley, I, still a young man, went West, out to Hollywood. And I do mean Hollywood, not Beverly Hills, not the Palisades, no 90210 for this kid. It was the part of Hollywood they always promise — promised to clean up and they never do, a part of Hollywood you see on Cops — where you twinkle and then wrinkle and people forget about you. That's where I'm from.

I swung into another clerk job, this time at CBS. I folded T-shirts in the gift shop, dusted off 60 Minutes mugs. Occasionally, after hours, I had conversations with the ghost of Bill Paley. It was during one of these wee-hour chats that he reminded me the first step in good reporting is good snooping. Inspired, I went out of my way to service the executive suites. I remember I delivered sweatshirts to Jeff Sagansky, at the time president of CBS.

Overhearing, listening to careful conversations, intercepting the occasional memo — [I] would volunteer in the mail room from time to time — I hit pay dirt when I discovered that the trash cans in the Xerox room at Television City were stuffed each morning with overnight Nielsen ratings — information gold. I don't know what I did with it. I guess we were — me and my friends knew Dallas had got a 35-share over Falcon Crest. But we thought we were plugged in.

I was on the move — least I thought so. But my father worried I was in a giant stall. And in a parental panic he overcame his fear of flying and dropped in for a visit. At the end of his stay, during the drive to the airport, sensing some action was called for, he dragged me into a blown-out strip on Sunset Boulevard and found a Circuit City store. "Come on," he said desperately. "I'm getting you a computer." "Oh, yeah, and what am I doing to do with that?" I laughed.

And as they say at CBS studies: "Cut, two months later." Having found a way to post things on the Internet — it was a quick learn; Internet news groups were very good to me early on — I moved on to scoops from the sound stages I had heard — Jerry Seinfeld asking for a million dollars an episode — to scoop after scoop of political things I had heard from some friends back here.

I collected a few e-mail addresses of interest. People had suggested I start a mailing list, so I collected the e-mails and set up a list called The Drudge Report. One reader turned into five, then turned into 100. And faster than you could say "I never had sex with that woman," it was 1,000, 5,000, 100,000 people! The ensuing website practically launched itself!

Last month I had 6 million visitors, and I currently have a daily average larger than the weekly newsstand sales of Time Magazine. Thank you, Sidney Blumenthal.

What's going on here? Well, clearly there is a hunger for unedited information, absent corporate considerations. As the first guy who has made a name for himself on the Internet, I've been invited to more and more high-toned gatherings such as this, the last being a conference on Internet & Society and some word I couldn't pronounce, up at Harvard a week ago. And I mention this not just to blow my own horn, but to make a point. Exalted minds — the panelists' and the audience's average IQ exceeds the Dow Jones — didn't appear to have a clue what this Internet's going to do; what we're going to make of it, what we're going to — what this is all going to turn into. But I have glimpses.

And sometimes deep in the middle of the night I tell them to Bill Paley.

We have entered an era vibrating with the din of small voices. Every citizen can be a reporter, can take on the powers that be. The difference between the Internet, television and radio, magazines, newspapers is the two-way communication. The Net gives as much voice to a 13-year-old computer geek like me as to a CEO or speaker of the House. We all become equal. And you would be amazed what the ordinary guy knows.

From a little corner in my Hollywood apartment, in the company of nothing more than my 486 computer and my six — six-toed cat, I have consistently been able to break big stories, thanks to this network of ordinary guys. The Drudge Report: first to name the vice-presidential nominee on the Republican ticket last election; first to announce to an American audience that Princess Diana had tragically died; first to sell — tell the sad, sad story of Kathleen Willey; first every weekend with box-office results that even studio executives, some of them, admit they get from me. A new cable network is forming. I was first to announce the unholy alliance between Microsoft and NBC.

I've written thousands of stories, started hundreds of news cycles. My readers can follow earthquakes, weather patterns, read Frank Rich on Saturday, Maureen Dowd on Sunday, from my site link to Bob Novak on Monday; dozens of other media spectrum[s], from Molly Ivins; track the world's news wires minute to minute.

And this is something new. This marks the first time that an individual has access to the news wires outside of a newsroom. You get to read all the news from the Associated Press, UPI, Reuters, to the more — the more arcane Agence France-Presse and the Xinhua. I'm a personal fan of the Xinhua Press.

And time was only newsrooms had access to the full pictures of the day's events. But now any citizen does. We get to see the kinds of cuts that are made for all kinds of reasons — endless layers of editors with endless agendas changing bits and pieces, so by the time the newspaper hits your welcome mat it had no meaning. Now with a modem, anyone can follow the world and report on the world — no middle man, no Big Brother. And I guess this changes everything.

It certainly changed on the night of January 17th, when Newsweek spiked, at the 11th hour, a well-researched, responsibly documented piece about the President of the United States and an obscure White House intern named Monica Lewinsky. After checking with multiple sources, I ran a story about the killing of the story. According to the Los Angeles Times, people familiar with the matter said Clinton was informed Saturday night or Sunday morning The Drudge Report had posted that Lewinsky was about to erupt. For four days I had the story exclusively, and I took a lot of heat. Everyone was afraid of it until the water broke...over at The Washington Post that Wednesday, and then everyone jumped on it.

Now they love it too much, and I'm still taking the heat. "He's one man out of control," a caller warned on talk radio in Los Angeles. "There is such a built-in level of irresponsibility in everything he does," cried First Amendment protector Floyd Abrams in a page one Wall Street Journal piece. "The notion of a Matt Drudge cyber gossip sitting next to William Safire on Meet the Press would have been unthinkable," smacked Watergate's Carl Bernstein in an op-ed.

I was here last night looking over the Press Club, and I noticed a room dedicated to one of — someone I can relate to, John Peter Zenger. And there's a plaque outside the room. And I think he could relate to some of the heat I've been getting:

To honor members of the newspaper industry, this room commemorates the achievements of John Peter Zenger 250 years ago, whose courage in publishing political criticism helped establish the precedent of press freedom in colonial America. He was born in Germany. Zenger was a publisher in 1734 when he was imprisoned on charges of criminal libel for articles in his newspaper criticizing the royal governor. Risking his business and possible life, Zenger stood fast and was acquitted in a jury trial after a brilliant defense of press liberty by his lawyer, at that time Andrew Hamilton.

Got me thinking that really what we're looking at here is history repeating. When radio lost out to television, there was anxiety. The people in the radio business were absolutely anxious and demanded government stop the upcoming television wave. Television was very nervous about other mediums coming forward — cable. The movies were — didn't want sitcoms to be taped at movie studios for fear it would take away from the movies.

No, television saved the movies. The Internet is going to save the news business. I — I envision a — a future where there'll be 300 million reporters, where anyone from anywhere can report for any reason. It's freedom of — freedom of participation, absolutely realized.

The First Lady of the United States recently addressed concerns about Internet during a Cyberspatial Millennium Project press conference just weeks after Lewinsky broke. She said,
We're all going to have to rethink how we deal with the Internet. As exciting as these new developments are, there are a number of serious issues without any kind of editing function or gatekeeping function.

I wonder who she was referring to.

Mrs. Clinton continued,

Any time an individual leaps so far ahead of that balance and throws a system, whatever it might be — political, economic, technological — out of balance, you've got a problem. It can lead to all kinds of bad outcomes which we have seen historically.

Would she have said the same thing about Ben Franklin or Thomas Edison or Henry Ford or Einstein? They all leapt so far ahead out that they shook the balance. No, I say to these people, faster, not slower. Create. Let your mind flow. Let the imagination take over. And if technology has finally caught up with individual liberty, why would anyone who loves freedom want to rethink that?

And that's why I'm addressing you today. It got me in the door, this new technology. You walk into the Press Club, you see a plaque dedicated to Joseph Pulitzer — someone, again, I love:

Our Republic and its press will rise or fall together. An able, disinterested, public-spirited press...can preserve that public virtue without which popular government is a sham and a mockery...The power to mold the future of the republic will be in the hands of the journalists of the future generations.

And if Pulitzer were alive today in this time, he would add "using future mediums."

I was walking the streets of Washington — the streets I grew up in — last night. Found myself in front of the Washington Post building again, looking up, this time not longingly. This time I laughed.

Let the future begin.

CHAPTER 10

EAST MEETS WEST — THE SHOWDOWN

Oh, East is East, and West is West,
and never the twain shall meet,
Till Earth and Sky stand presently
at God's great Judgment Seat;
But there is neither East nor West,
Border, nor Breed, nor Birth,
When two strong men stand face to face,
though they come from the ends of the earth!
— From the poem 'The Ballad of East
and West' by Rudyard Kipling

1979

Sun Myung Moon's Divine Principle states that the Second Coming, like the First, will occur through natural childbirth. Furthermore, it will take place in the Far East[1]

---

1 Exposition of the Divine Principle, Chapter 6, Section 3.2: The Lion of the tribe of Judah signifies Christ; it is he who will open the seven seals in the Last Days. After six of the seals are opened:
   Then I saw another angel ascend from the rising of the sun, with the seal of the living God, and he called with a loud voice . . . saying, "Do not harm the earth or the sea or the trees, till we have sealed the servants of our God upon their foreheads." And I heard the number of the sealed, a hundred and forty-four thousand. -Rev. 7:2-4
   [https://www.biblegateway.com/passage/?search=Revelation+7&language=en&version=CEV]
   This indicates that the seal of the living God will be placed on the foreheads of the 144,000 in the East, where the sun rises. These chosen ones will accompany the Lamb at his

and "will come like a thief."

This doctrine of course flies in the face of theological conventions of all stripes. But it also underscores the mystery of the Orient for Occidentals.

The cultural divide between East and West is profound also within the spiritual movement inspired by Sun Myung Moon.

The Far East is seen in the West as sometimes exotic, sometimes ominous or threatening as in the "yellow peril."[2]

For the U.S. military, the Pacific Theater in World War II followed by the Korean War and the Vietnam War underscored the formidable, if hidden power in the Far East. Thus Gen. Douglas MacArthur famously warned John F. Kennedy against committing ground troops in Vietnam. This was after MacArthur had been fired by President Harry Truman for publicly advocating his insistence on outflanking the North Korean and Chinese troops as a strategy to win the Korean War in which American troops were being overwhelmed by the sheer numbers of Chinese invaders. He was fired, but returned to the U.S. as a hero, notably in the eyes of the young and rising JFK[3].

---

return.73(Rev. 14:1) [https://www.biblegateway.com/passage/?search=Revelation+14&language=en&version=KJV] We can thus infer that the nation which will inherit the work of God and bear its fruit for the sake of the Second Advent is in the East. There Christ will be born and received by the 144,000 elect of God.

2   According to Wikipedia: "The Yellow Peril (also the Yellow Terror and the Yellow Specter) is a racial color metaphor that depicts the peoples of East and Southeast Asia as an existential danger to the Western world. As a psychocultural menace from the Eastern world, fear of the Yellow Peril is racial, not national, fear derived not from concern with a specific source of danger from any one people or country, but from a vaguely ominous, existential fear of the faceless, nameless hordes of yellow people.

3   'MacArthur's Last Stand Against a Winless War,' Mark Parry, October 3, 2018. The Ameri-

President John F. Kennedy with General Douglas MacArthur at the White House on Aug. 16, 1962. / Abbie Rowe, White House Photographs / John F Kennedy Library / Public Domain

The 1953 ceasefire in the Korean War brought a truce and the infamous Demilitarized Zone (DMZ). Thus, the war had still not ended as this is written in 2022.

Significantly, a precedent was established for the American military, the greatest in world history, of essentially surrendering in Asian theaters.

The term "yellow peril" was first used in relation to the waves of Chinese immigrants in the 1800s that delivered cheap labor for the nation-building transcontinental railroads and cost jobs for white Americans.[4] The Japanese

can Conservative: https://www.theamericanconservative.com/macarthurs-last-stand-against-a-winless-war/. "MacArthur's warning about fighting in Asia impressed Kennedy, who repeated it in the months ahead and especially whenever military leaders urged him to take action. "Well now," the young president would say in his lilting New England twang, "you gentlemen, you go back and convince General MacArthur, then I'll be convinced."

4   According to Wikipedia: The history of Chinese Americans or the history of ethnic Chinese in the United States includes three major waves of Chinese immigration to the United

immigrants came later to Hawaii and the West Coast, following the Meiji Restoration (from feudalism to centralized
imperial rule) in 1868 which marked the end of the Tokugawa
shogunate in Japan.

Significant Korean immigration to America did not really
begin until after the Korean War. According to Wikipedia:

> After the annexation of Korea by Japan in 1910, Korean
> migration to the United States was virtually halted.
> The Immigration Act of 1924 or sometimes referred to
> as the *Oriental Exclusion Act* was part of a measured
> system excluding Korean immigrants into the US. ...
> With the passage of the Immigration and Nationality
> Act of 1965, Koreans became one of the fastest growing
> Asian groups in the United States. ... Large numbers of
> Koreans, including some from North Korea who had
> come via South Korea, have been immigrating ever since,
> putting Korea in the top six countries of origin of immi-
> grants to the United States since 1975. The reasons for
> immigration are many including the desire for
> increased freedom and the hope for better economic
> opportunities.[5]

States, beginning in the 19th century. Chinese immigrants in the 19th century worked as
laborers, particularly on transcontinental railroads such as the Central Pacific Railroad. They
came not only for the gold rush in California, but were also hired to help build the First
Transcontinental Railroad. They also worked as laborers in mining, and suffered racial
discrimination at every level of society. Industrial employers were eager for this new and
cheap labor. This resulted in many white people losing their jobs and were stirred to anger
by the «yellow peril.» .... So hostile was the opposition that in 1882 the United States Congress passed the Chinese Exclusion Act prohibiting immigration from China for the following ten years. This law was then extended by the Geary Act in 1892. The Chinese Exclusion
Act is seen by some as the only U.S. law ever to prevent immigration and naturalization on
the basis of race.

5 Wikipedia: Another prominent figure among the Korean immigrant community was Syn-
gman Rhee (이승만), a Methodist.[2] He came to the United States in 1904 and earned

Thus was the stage set for the advent of Sun Myung Moon from the East to the West in the Twentieth Century. A rocky reception was in the forecast. But the East-West divide was also a momentous challenge within his own church and related businesses in the United States.

In 1979, while working as the Tokyo correspondent for the New York daily newspaper that paved the way for The Washington Times, I learned that trouble was brewing back at the home office.

Operating in an era before cell phones, the Internet and email, I filed my stories daily either from UPI where I had a desk, phone and file cabinet or via telex from our sister newspaper, Sekai Nippo in the Shibuya section of Tokyo. So, through letters, cryptic messages and rare phone calls I had learned of power struggles involving the newspaper's leadership including the publisher, Michael Young Warder, a Stanford graduate.

My limited professional experiences with Warder had all been positive. He communicated economically, making clear his policy expectations without interfering in the editorial process. He supported my reporting about the presence of IRS officials in their own office at the Unification Church headquarters on 4 West 43rd St. [Chapter 7, The IRS Office at UC Headquarters]. That initial report got both of us in trouble with the church hierarchy. However, we later learned that the Founder had not been upset about the report. Quite the opposite.

a bachelor's degree at George Washington University in 1907, a master's degree at Harvard University, and a Ph.D. from Princeton University in 1910. In 1910, he returned to Korea and became a political activist. He later became the first president of the Republic of Korea.

The first foreshadowing of the coming East-West show-down at News World Communications, which published the New York daily and later The Washington Times, had come shortly after I was appointed Tokyo correspondent in the autumn of 1977. Warder wanted me to arrive in Japan on Dec. 7 (the 36th anniversary of Japan's surprise attack on Pearl Harbor) "to send a signal." Because my visa did not come through in time and I was involved in unfinished reporting projects, I could not leave until 1978. But his directive about my arrival date was the first clue that he saw problems ahead from the predominantly Japanese and Korean hierarchy in the Unification movement, leaders of which had seniority over Americans like Warder.

Later in Japan, I heard from my colleagues in New York that the newspaper's coverage was criticized by the Founder for being out of touch with the realities of international communism as played out in U.S. politics. I found myself sympathetic with this criticism from my experiences work-ing at the Daily Texan at the University of Texas, Austin, as a journalism graduate student and as a reporter in New York and Washington. My reporting experiences on the DMZ in Korea, the Narita Airport riots in Japan and in Taiwan and Iran reinforced the perspective of U.S. media bias ideolog-ically in synch with international communism. In Asia, communism was an existential, political and military reality whereas back home it was more of a mass psychological transformation phenomenon that played out culture-wide in the post-World War II era.

Most American journalists had a U.S.-centric worldview if they had a worldview at all. For average Americans there really is no reality outside the bubble of the continental U.S. experience. Tourism or brief visits abroad cannot challenge this perspective. Only going native in other nations for extended periods of time can awaken Americans to how things appear outside their sheltered cultural sphere.

The U.S. foreign correspondents I knew in Tokyo and Seoul in the late 1970s were news professionals cut from a mold that has become rare. Although living in relative isolation from the Japanese, they cultivated original sources, verified reports and questioned authority. However, their shared perspective on the context of the news was grounded in U.S. embassy sources and generally left-of-center politics which always struck me as odd. Chinese, Soviet and North Korean communism was a geopolitical reality in East Asia and yet liberal anti-American biases were still in vogue with the American press corps after the disastrous conclusion of the Vietnam War.

One morning in Tokyo, I was at the Foreign Correspondent Club when word came from the Foreign Press Center that a group of Vietnamese "boat people" who had been rescued at sea by a Japanese vessel would be arriving that afternoon in Tokyo Bay. The foreign press was invited to join their Japanese colleagues in reporting this news. "Let's go," I said. But none of my colleagues were interested. I was the lone American correspondent to meet the arrivals who as it turned out had stories to tell rich in "human interest" and which formed the basis for a 4-part series I wrote on "Vietnam's Boat People". One young man I met and stayed in contact with over the years had been a photographer in the Saigon Bureau of the Washington Post.

Meanwhile, a full-scale revolt was brewing back in New York that would permanently split the newsroom. The editor, John Dolen, contacted me personally. He confided that he planned to leave the newspaper and that he hoped I would return and replace him. A fiery Korean man, Sung San Lee, had been appointed as the owner's representative and was shaking things up. [See Chapter 8] Lee spoke relatively good broken English and had worked for U.S. military intelligence in Korea. It was 1979, Jimmy Carter was president, and the Soviet Union was winning the Cold War. Lee's message to the newspaper's American leadership was that journalism is war and their editorial mission was to fight the spread of international communism which continued to penetrate all aspects of American life. Unsophisticated in the ways of the West, he was regarded as a bull in the China shop.

The energetic and articulate Michael Warder was quite the opposite in terms of style. Ideologically, he favored a center right perspective. He contacted me in the summer of 1979 and asked that I set up meetings for him with South Korean government officials in Seoul in his capacity as Publisher of the News World and Secretary General of the International Conference on the Unity of Science (a church-related organization dedicated to the unity of science and religion).

During a late-night meeting at the Lotte Hotel in Seoul where we were staying, he confided to me about the struggles he was facing as an American dealing with a Unification Church hierarchy comprised of Korean and Japanese "elders" and disciples of Sun Myung Moon. He regarded Lee as a change agent preparing the way he said for another Korean to represent the Founder's interests in his first American newspaper. "Bo Hi

Pak," he correctly predicted, "will be sitting in my chair one year from now."

According to Wikipedia,

> Pak was a lieutenant colonel in the South Korean military when he joined the Unification Church in the 1950s. Serving church founder Sun Myung Moon as his main English interpreter during speaking tours in the United States, he was referred to in the media as Moon‹s «right-hand man" . . . .He was the central figure in Moon's publishing businesses, including founding President and Publisher, *The News World* (later renamed *New York City Tribune*); founding President and Chairman of the Board, the Washington Times Corporation; and President, World Media Association.

I shared with Warder my observations gained from working with and frequently debating Japanese colleagues at Sekai Nippo most of whom were church members. I compared the plight of "round eyes" like him and me with the solar system. The Asians, I told him were in the inner orbits, like Mercury and Venus in the Unification movement's hierarchy. Westerners on the other hand were in the outer orbits and further from the sun. There was no changing this reality I had concluded.

The next morning at breakfast, Warder told me he had thought about what I said. "You're wrong," he said simply with a smile. A few months later, when I returned to New York for the "World Media Conference" sponsored by our newspaper, Warder had just resigned. I subsequently heard that Sun Myung Moon was heartbroken by Warder's decision.

In subsequent private meetings with Warder and other

non-Unification Church media officials at The Washington Times and the Spanish language Noticias del Mundo, I shared my perspective and insights. Forget about winning arguments, I advised. In the life-and-death struggle on the media battlefield, the foe is principalities, not people. Unificationists, like communists, are invested long-term. From that perspective, quitting is worse than death and not an option.

Warder left with animus, and his departure marked the end of significant Western leadership in the Unification Movement. The latter became an Oriental splinter in the unwelcoming body politic of the United States. Subsequent Korean-born owner's representatives at The Washington Times and their American subordinates worked tirelessly for success, but as the expression goes, they were "pissing into the wind."

As explained elsewhere, I was never directly involved in church activities. However, it was my observation that the same East-West divide was never resolved within that spiritual community despite heroic efforts on both sides of the cultural divide.

Had Sun Myung Moon's message taken root and thrived in the United States, the impact on his own family who were raised and educated there and on his global stature would have been significant.

CHAPTER 11

THE UNNATURAL 'SUSPENSION' OF THE NYC TRIBUNE

1991

January 4, 1991 marked the end of a years-long uphill battle to properly launch the New York City Tribune. Remarkably, that launch never happened. This daily newspaper was on life support from the day in 1983 that The News World changed its name to the New York Tribune.

Give a thought to a metropolitan daily newspaper that never had an independent business management operation.

The New York Times sued the New York Tribune over its new name [Chapter 5, 'Start spreading the news']. Rather than enter the fight, which I argued we could win and that would in any case provide free publicity for our publishing venture, the management opted to cave. We became the New York City Tribune.

The management team at the offices at 401 Fifth Ave. in New York City were focused not on the Tribune but rather on the Spanish language newspaper chain, Noticias del Mundo, (in New York, Los Angeles and Miami), the Continental real estate group and Stellar Printing (in Long Island City) because they were regarded as a potentially

NEW YORK CITY TRIBUNE BUILDING
HEADQUARTERS OF NEWS WORLD COMMUNICATIONS, INC.

viable business concerns. Furthermore, this team reported to Bo Hi Pak at The Washington Times who viewed the New York paper as a competitor for urgently-needed subsidies and that should be closed, immediately if not sooner.

There was clear-cut logic to that perspective. Like others who worked under him, I liked and admired "Col. Pak" (later known as Dr. Pak) who was key to the miraculous launch of The Washington Times under the alpha male force and funding of its Founder, Sun Myung Moon.[1] I was told that some rank and file Unification Church members regarded the suspension of the NYC Tribune as either a good thing or of no consequence.

So here you had the anomaly of a New York City newspaper supported by its Founder but not by many of his followers.[2]

Founded on the last day of 1976 as The News World, it had been the top daily in New York City during the newspaper strike of 1978. Home on leave from Tokyo where I was the correspondent, I was thrilled while riding the subway to see many people reading our newspaper on a day when one of my articles from Japan had been published on page one.

Our Washington bureau team, headed by Josette Sheeran, transferred to The Washington Times with its 1982 launch. I remained behind as the editor of the scaled-back New York Tribune.

Thus began a quiet but fierce internal newspaper war waged in two cities over scarce financial resources generated at great sacrifice by other business interests established by Sun Myung Moon. Editorially, the New York daily won several major awards including those by star reporters Cheryl Smith Wetzstein and Peter Klebnikov. Peter came from a

---

1   When The Washington Times was launched in 1982, the widespread profession view, privately expressed, was that the paper could not survive more than six months in the harsh media-political environment.

2   Part II will provide more detail on the high-level internal debate (known only to those who participated) about the value of the New York newspaper in the News World Communications, Inc. media group.

prominent family of Russian descent and had interned at the New York Times.[3] As also noted in Chapter 5, the Tribune was responsible for a long list of exclusives including his first assignment — special reports on the organized crime connections of the husband of Democrat Vice Presidential nominee Geraldine Ferraro.

The New York Tribune also launched the column writing career of Mayor Ed Koch.

During an interview with our editors at his office, I informed the mayor that one of our columnists opposed his policies. "Who?" he asked. "Betty Wein", I replied.

"Oh Betty," he sighed. "She hates me." Betty Wein headed an organization called Morality in Media. She championed family values which were not a priority for liberal Democrats like Ed Koch.

I reminded the mayor that our large Commentary section was open to everyone who could write a publishable column, from taxi drivers to the mayor of New York City. Koch accepted on the spot and wrote weekly from that point, and subsequently for other newspapers as well.

Liberal Democrats like Ed Koch were not among the core NYC Tribune constituencies which included the following:

- Recent immigrants from Soviet bloc nations for whom communism was a hard reality, not an abstraction. This community flocked to a debate at the

---

3 Klebnikov's great-grandfather, an admiral in the White Russian fleet, was assassinated by the Bolsheviks. His brother Paul headed the Moscow edition of Forbes Magazine when he was tragically assassinated in 2004 in a major blow to investigative journalism in post-Soviet Russia.

Waldorf Astorial Hotel between a no-show New York Times editor and our columnist Lev Navrozov who nevertheless got a raucous reception as he decimated his absent opponent.

- Sub-sections of the large Arts community in New York City that rebelled against the Marxist-nihilist influences that gave rise to such abominations as Andres Serrano's "Piss Christ".

- Reagan conservatives, a persecuted minority in Manhattan but a powerful underground force in other boroughs and especially out on Long Island.

One young man, from Long Island visited my office on March 21, 1990, and liked what he saw and the people he met including our resident émigré firebrand Lev Navrozov. He was a schoolteacher in the Bronx who had recently earned his master's degree from the London School of Economics. His name was Chris Ruddy, who would later create and head Newsmax Media.

A new friend and occasional guest at our apartment in West Harrison, N.Y., Chris had a goal. He wanted the NYC Tribune to establish a branch operation in Long Island as part of his "Alternative to Newsday" campaign to counter the liberal-left dominant newspaper. To that end, we established a weekly section for Long Island readers and had meetings with our new constituency many of whom were conservative Catholics, Jews and Democrats as well as, of course, the Nassau County Republican Party.

All of these positive developments fell on deaf ears back at 401 Fifth Ave. where the senior management continued to resist funding even the most basic business functions of the newspaper. The fact that the Tribune was on the move despite lack of internal support may have hastened its suspension.

Over the Christmas holidays of 1990, I was told that the end was imminent. As the responsible editor from the first day until the last, the news came as a devastating blow, akin to losing a child. But it was not the end. The New York City Tribune "suspended" publication on January 4, 1991.

Words have meanings. "Suspended" is the correct term, not death.

I later learned that the decision was based on unrelenting pressure from the Founder's subordinates and an audit based on false premises, namely that the bulk of the subsidies for the "New York City Tribune" division of News World Communications was consumed by the newspaper. In fact, the reverse was true: The lion's share of the funding went to the Noticias del Mundo newspaper operations (with its New York, L.A. and Miami editions), the commercial printing business and the Continental Real Estate venture.

None of those entities were in the black financially, but only the Tribune suspended operations. At the same time, the Tribune took the blame internally for the roughly 5 percent of the subsidy pie that was not going to Washington. The D.C. operations had grown to include Insight magazine, Atlantic Video broadcast facilities and the Nostalgia Network cable property.

The daily newspaper and its key supporters could have been viewed as a cost-effective strategic resource for the media group and the significant New York conservative

The New York Times

N.Y. / Region
Tribune Suspends Publication
Published: January 5, 1991

community including on Long Island, not to mention the Founder himself whose residence was in Westchester County, New York.

As mentioned earlier [see Chapter 3], Sun Myung Moon subsequently assured me privately that the newspaper would resume publication and that many others would be established throughout the United States and the world. At a small meeting in the Washington Times in 1997 with his representative, Dong Moon Joo, I learned that the Founder was still committed to that vision.

Without a business division, the suspension of the NYC Tribune would seem inevitable. But who am I to say that what the Founder envisioned should be terminated?

I remained convinced that his concept of the newspaper as an alternative to the Marxist New York Times, with an international focus and editorial emphasis on both the "Culture War" and the "War of Ideas," was not only valid but critical.

Years later, acting independently from what remained of the Sun Myung Moon media group, I founded WorldTribune.com as America's first daily digital newspaper that gives priority to geopolitics and culture.

What follows is the NY Times' report on its last real

competitor in the New York metropolitan area and the story of the New York City Tribune's remarkable decade marked by its motto: "Rise of a New Era".

The New York City Tribune, a Monday-through-Friday newspaper founded by the Rev. Sun Myung Moon in 1976, suspended publication yesterday. The paper's paid circulation, which reached a peak of 400,000 during the newspaper strike of 1978, had dwindled to 12,000, said Thomas D. Zumbo, the associate editor. News World Communications, which owns The Tribune, described the suspension as a temporary "rest" forced by a poor economy.

According to Wikipedia,

a "new" *New York Tribune* debuted in 1976 in New York City. The paper, which was originally named *The News World* and later changed to *The New York City Tribune*, was published by News World Communications, Inc., owned by the Unification Church. It was published in the former Tiffany and Company Building at 401 Fifth Avenue until it printed its last edition on January 3, 1991.[11] Its sister paper, *The Washington Times*, is circulated primarily in the nation's capital. The *Tribune* carried an expansive «Commentary» section of opinions and editorials. Former New York City Mayor Ed Koch was one of the columnists.

CHAPTER 12

THE WASHINGTON TIMES: 'AMERICA'S NEWSPAPER' UNTIL IT WASN'T

1982

Founded in 1982, The Washington Times would continue to be recognized as a crowning achievement for its Founder well into the 21st Century.

Motorcade for former Israeli Prime Minister Benjamin Netanyahu at The Washington Times on April 10, 2002. / Mary Calvert / The Washington Times

The Times filled a void early in the Ronald Regan Administration left by the death of the Washington Star in 1981. As I would explain to visitors after joining The Times in late 1991, the Star's demise shortly after Ronald Reagan's election (against the advice of the U.S. media establishment) had been devastating.

In those days, most big city American and foreign newspapers had offices at the National Press Club building on 14th St. NW. Bureau chiefs and correspondents would rely on the "daybook" provided by the major wire services (AP and UPI) as the menu for their daily coverage. But it was the Washington Post at their office doors every morning that provided the real agenda and context the worldwide press corps relied upon to plan their news coverage. With the death of the Star, the power of the Washington Post was unchallenged in those days before the Internet and cable news.

What about President Ronald Reagan's agenda that included cutting taxes and overturning the Soviet Union's looming military and strategic dominance? It faced a hostile Washington bureaucracy and had virtually no media support despite his landslide victory after a bitterly fought campaign.

The arrival of "the Cavalry" came in the form of The Washington Times, staffed by some of the best of the Washington Star news professionals and many others.

Suddenly, there it was, delivered daily to all those bureaus of the U.S. and foreign press at the National Press Club. Now there was the other side of the big stories of the day as well as other major stories that the liberal media would never think of covering.

In the days before instant online information, The Washington Times helped restore the critical debate in the public forum required for American democracy to function properly.

For this, The Washington Times and its founder were never forgiven by the growing totalitarian force in American politics and culture which I refer to simply as "The Left". Go to Wikipedia and search for The Washington Times and you will find none of its notable editorial exclusives such as the House Banking and Post Office scandals of the early 1990s or the "call boy" sex scandals of the late 1980s that ensnarled prominent politicians of both parties and including the Reagan and Bush administrations and even prominent journalists.[1]

But The Washington Times found its way into the daily political discourse and news coverage during the next two decades even though it was rarely properly credited for its exclusives. Rush Limbaugh and conservative commentators referred to its coverage almost with reverence, assuming that everyone knew how important this newspaper was. The National Weekly Edition telegraphed this influence and authoritativeness nationwide. In private conversations with other conservative publishers that decades later had

---

1   https://en.wikipedia.org/wiki/House_banking_scandal
    https://en.wikipedia.org/wiki/Congressional_Post_Office_scandal   1991-95
    Michael Hedges and Jerry Seper, "Power broker served drugs, sex at parties bugged for blackmail" The Washington Times June 30, 1989
    Paul M. Rodriguez and George Archibald, "Homosexual prostitution inquiry ensnares VIPs with Reagan, Bush" The Washington Times June 29, 1989
    Frank J. Murray, "White House mute on 'call boy' probe" The Washington Times July 7, 1989
    Michael Hedges and Jerry Seper, "Spence's death result of drug, alcohol poisoning" The Washington Times Jan 3, 1990

hoped to topple The Times from its perch, I was told that
its brand was formidable and an obstacle to achieving their
goals.

As mentioned in Chapter 4, The Times' special insights
into the Clinton White House and Jerry Seper's award-winning reporting about the Whitewater scandal reinforced
the Times' reputation earned during its glory days of the
Reagan era.

The Times' national security coverage by Bill Gertz,
Rowan Scarborough and others made the newspaper a
must-read at the Pentagon, the intelligence agencies,
Embassy Row and worldwide. Former Defense Secretary
Donald Rumsfeld and former intelligence chiefs spoke of
reading reports by Gertz to remain plugged in from the
outside after returning to the private sector. There can be
no question that The Times' news, commentary and editorials were key to the Reagan Administration's success in
ending the Soviet Union's bid for global hegemony.

The larger-than-life personality responsible for marshal-
ing The Washington Times from ideal to reality was Col.
Bo Hi Pak, a Korean War veteran who had worked under
American officers during that conflict which to this day
remains unresolved. He had a booming voice and a command of English enhanced by his work ethic and careful
study of American orators. As the leading translator and
disciple of Sun Myung Moon, he provided essential repre-
sentation for a native North Korean whose uncompromis-
ing style clashed with the ways of Washington and mystified
many Americans including Unification Church members.
With his phenomenal rolodex in Washington, DC, Col.

Pak was a key ingredient in the secret sauce that helped The Washington Times achieve its two decades of glory.

Hundreds of others, including former Washington Star staffers, prominent conservative journalists, commentators

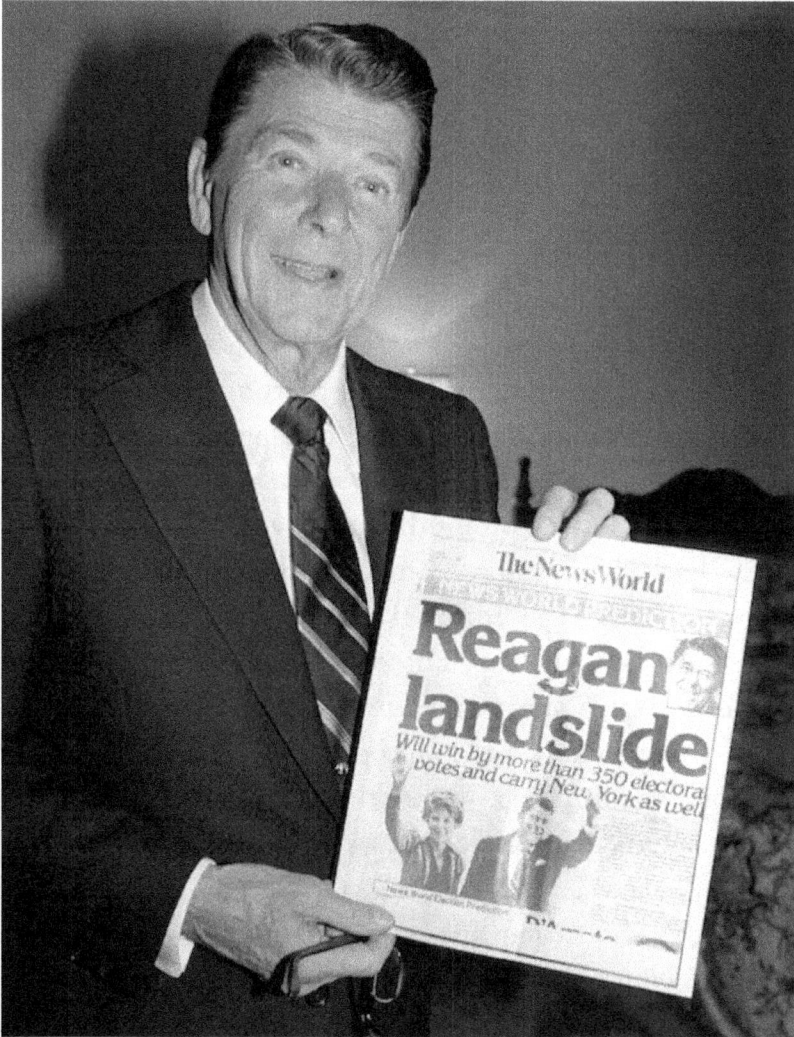

The News World 1980 election day edition led with a bold prediction. — The News World

and Unification Church members would subsequently play critical roles. All of course were tainted by association with the "Moonies" and the Koreans and would later often remove references to The Times from their resumes.

I was a member of the small team in New York that debated, clashed and spent late nights drawing up Plans A and B for the launching of what became known in the 1990s as "America's Newspaper". Key members of this group were at the Washington bureau of the New York branch of News World Communications, and its unofficial leader was Josette Sheeran.

Josette came from a prominent Catholic family in New Jersey and was a natural in terms of personality, savvy and looks. Her degree was in journalism from the University of Colorado, but she was destined for bigger things.

My close friend Jonathan Slevin was the son of a Jewish father and a Protestant mother both with prominent newspaper backgrounds as were other relatives including Anthony Day, Editorial Page Editor at the Los Angeles Times.

Ted Agres and Paula Hunker both came from Jewish families. Paula, short in stature, was brilliant with a firecracker personality and could pull off just about anything she put her mind to. When the New York News World published its historic election day "Reagan Landslide" edition, Paula was assigned the news analysis behind the headline. She froze. "Don't think about it, just do it," I advised. She did, with finesse, in an edition that was jubilantly held aloft by Reagan as the votes were coming in after being presented a copy by Washington bureau chief Josette Sheeran.

After being promoted to Managing Editor by Editor in Chief Wesley Pruden in the early 1990s, Josette would later leave The Washington Times for executive positions first at the State Department in 2005, and subsequently at the World Health Organization and the Asia Society.

Ted Agres, who over the years became my best friend, had graduated from the University of Chicago and continued to write freelance for science publications while working his newspaper day jobs. Ted has partnered with me in several investigative reporting[2] and publishing ventures. An excellent writer and facile editor, Ted was assigned to a primarily administrative role in The Washington Times newsroom where he was a reassuring presence offering counsel and assistance to stressed reporters and editors who excelled with his support.

I came from Protestant Christian parents, the grandson on my father's side of a saintly minister whose gift of pocket New Testament is still in my laptop bag for good luck. After writing a humor column and working as layout editor for my college newspaper, I had transferred from the mathematics graduate program at the University of Texas to its School of Communications. Never intending to actually work in journalism, that profession had become my destiny [See Chapter 2].

When The Washington Times launched in 1982, these four friends (Josette, Jonathan, Paula and Ted) were on site as Pak's lieutenants (known subsequently in the Times newsroom as the "Gang of Four") and played key roles in

---

2   See Chapter 5 on the series "Subversion in Washington: The Radical Network That's Infil-trated The White House"

what history should record as an epochal event in American journalism. I stayed behind in New York as the editor in chief of the New York City Tribune where the prototype editions of The Times were published.

Later after moving to Washington, I proposed, helped Art Director Gil Roschuni design and then edited the National Weekly Edition of The Times beginning on the 50th anniversary of D-Day on June 6, 1994. The National Weekly also launched The Times' first Internet editions. In the days before social media and cable news, we delivered exclusive daily news coverage from the left-leaning Nation's Capital to more receptive audiences outside the beltway "from sea to shining sea."

"America's Newspaper" was an organic part of the National Weekly's logo until a focus group in Northern Virginia objected to the slogan as presumptuous during a misguided repositioning of The Times in 2008. Later, after the paper had lost traction amid the new alternative media revolution, it returned.

By early 2013 when I left The Times, my four friends were long gone, and The Times was a shadow of its former self. What happened? Ask any former or current employee and you will get a different answer. Ultimately, most media organizations have become subsidized operations that are not sustainable. Cut the funding and the impact is gone.

The Times continues to do outstanding work, particularly with its national security coverage and commentary. And it's fair to say that The Washington Times is not alone. All once-great American newspapers are now empty shells with no commercial clout and declining influence.

Perhaps newspapers are dinosaurs in the "Information Age" when each citizen has become his or her own publisher via social media, as prophesied by Matt Drudge [see Chapter 9].

Perhaps the United States of American will not survive as a beacon of freedom, light and hope to the world.

I am pulling for the return of The Washington Times or a similar enterprise as a winning media force.

The nation and world need an authoritative and trusted "newspaper of record" to reinforce objective reality on the foundation of Judeo-Christian absolute values and to champion Truth with a capital T.

That after all is what this business is all about: "You shall know the Truth and the Truth shall set you free."[3]

---

3 John 8:32

CHAPTER 13

CHRIST ON EARTH: A NEWSWORTHY EVENT?

2023

What would people think of God living on Earth with Adam and Eve?

In the hyper-secular society of the early 21st century, such is regarded as a myth relegated to the Genesis account of the Garden of Eden in the Bible. Even believers do not necessarily endorse an earthly bond between God and humanity. The neo-Marxist "woke" revolution of the current era is rooted in erasing the very assumptions this concept is rooted in.

The separation or divorce between the human family and its Creator is a given. In polite society, one does not even speak of God or of Satan as actual beings with a stake in life on Earth.

From the perspective of believers, the coming of Jesus was a one-time event that ended badly after only 33 years. But his sacrifice and resurrection are regarded by Christians as the basis for eternal salvation albeit one that excludes planet Earth.

We are "saved" in Heaven after death but not on Earth. The "Second Coming" is subject to a variety of interpretations most of which do not include restoring the Garden of

(From Wikimedia public domain images and original photos)
https://www.jmbeatty.com/page11.html

Eden ideal on this planet even were humanity to survive the "last days".

The 2,100 years after Christ in Christian history were marked by the canonization of the Holy Bible which included the Gospels on the short life of Jesus and epistles concerning the early church in the first century A.D. The Bible, other than its vivid and timeless prophecies, is silent on the momentous events more than a hundred years after the earthly life of Jesus as Christianity spread from the early churches described in the New Testament to all corners of the World.

Were the series of wars involving Jerusalem and the expansion of the new faith to Rome and then to Europe and on to America part of Divine Providence?

Yes, according to Sun Myung Moon's Divine Principle which includes chapters on "Providential Time Identity". Charts with time periods of 120, 40 and 21 demonstrate parallels between the periods from Adam to Abraham's family, the Israelites' slavery and exodus as the chosen lineage culminating in the birth of Jesus, and finally the 2,000 years through Augustine, Charlemagne, Martin Luther, the World Wars and the Second Coming. Thus, God's providence of restoring His lost children took place with the same mathematical precision with which He created the universe, according to the Divine Principle.

In his worldwide ministry, Sun Myung Moon presented God, the Heavenly Father as aspiring to be the True Love partner of all people, His children. Because of the Fall and the violence done to God's Love and ideal, the Messiah would be necessary to start the lengthy process of restoring the lost connection, lifeline and lineage. But God's Providence writ large had always been delayed, time and again, by the failure of human responsibility necessitating the return of Christ on Earth.

As for the Second Coming, what would precede this apocalyptic event and what would it look like?

During the Christian era, missionaries delivered the Gospel throughout the world including the Far East. Thus, the stage was set, according to Sun Myung Moon.

That epochal event would occur naturally he said, like the first, beginning with the birth of a child.

For teaching this heresy, Sun Myung Moon was imprisoned and tortured in both North and South Korea where Christianity had emerged as the dominant cultural force in the 1940s and 1950s. But he continued to teach and preach to whomever would listen, always advising listeners to pray about what they had heard. A detailed and fascinating chronicle of his life-and-death experiences in war-torn Korea where competing spirit-filled churches were preparing for the Messiah was written exclusively by Seoul-based journalist Michael Breen (Sun Myung Moon, The Early Years, 1920-53). Breen relied solely on interviews with scores of sources who had come into contact with the young teacher. He did not cite church sources or literature.

Sun Myung Moon taught that the goal of the Second Messiah, like the first, would be to become "True Parents", who would be the origin of a new lineage on Earth, the Tree of Life, to restore the position of Adam and through him God's sovereignty on Earth.

This would be the fulfillment of Jesus' prayer, he taught: "Thy Kingdom come, thy will be done, on Earth as it is in Heaven."

That phrase from the "Lord's Prayer"[1] implies the obvious: The physical world is not currently God's home as born out in II Corinthians 4:4: "In their case, the god of this world has blinded the minds of those who do not believe to keep them from seeing the light of the glorious gospel of the Messiah, who is the image of God."

As Sun Myung Moon elaborated:

> In Buddhism and Christian thought, they think that God is omniscient and omnipotent and free to take life and give life and can pass judgment by giving punishments and blessings. They could never be so wrong. In this light, amongst the religions, the Unification Church embraces teachings of a higher dimension. Without doubt, it is a religion that labors to find solutions. ...

---

1 Matthew 6:9-13

Other than the Unification Church, there has never been a religion that is determined to liberate God.[2]

Perhaps the most receptive part of the world for his new Truth was Korea which before the southern half became a modern, affluent and secularized society and the northern half became communist, was known for embracing all religions.

As a foreign correspondent based in Tokyo, my first trip to Seoul in 1978 was memorable. As the plane descended to Gimpo Airport that night, the skyline was marked by dozens of steeples with lighted crosses. As if on cue, the hymn "Amazing Grace" from my childhood began playing in my mind's sound system.

Sun Myung Moon taught that the "Kingdom" which he and Jesus sought was to be achieved on Earth as well as in Heaven. Koreans were the new "chosen" people and a unified Korea was to be the chosen nation, the Fatherland and the beachhead for the Kingdom of God on Earth.

Here is how he explained it:

Meaning of Savior

What in the world is the savior?

What is the purpose of his coming? He is not coming to be a political leader. Why would a savior come? Christians today say that when the Lord comes, they will all rise up and be lifted into the sky, and those left on earth will be judged. That will not happen. That is not the reality.

They say he brings judgment, but the savior does not

---

2 Cheon Seong Gyeong: (233-270, 1992.8.2)

come to pass judgment. He comes as God's Son and also as the Parent of humankind.

Would the person who comes as the Parent of humankind, and with a parental heart, remove his sons and daughters who are groaning in illness and on the verge of death saying, "Hey you, go to hell!"? Even parents in the fallen world would choke with grief and sorrow to see their children dying in such a miserable state. Their heart would compel them to do anything to save their children, even if they lose their own life. If that is how the parents in the fallen world are, how much more so would it be for the Savior who comes with the heart of the original Parent? Judgment would be unthinkable. Isn't that so?[3]

Role of South Koreans

First, the Parents should be attended in South Korea. They should be attended better than the North Koreans attend Kim Il-Sung. North Koreans carry Kim Il-Sung badges.

Unificationists should not be ashamed and stand even more proudly before the world than they do. North Koreans are all armed with Juche (self-reliance) thought. So, we should arm ourselves with the Three Subjects Principle centered on God's unshakable and absolute love and widen the gap with the North Koreans so that they cannot interfere with us. Walking such a path is our mission.[4]

---

3 Cheon Seong Gyeong: (222-150, 1991.11.3)
4 Cheon Seong Gyeong: (212-56, 1991.1.1)

North Korea's False Father

Kim Il-Sung is the false father. North Koreans call him their parent, do they not? Why has he appeared at this time in history? The person who is the most villainous in all the communist countries, the greatest of all devils, will appear.

However, I am called the True Parent. The True Parent should be able to subjugate the false parent through natural surrender. He should not be struck down by force.

God's providence of salvation and God's victory or defeat is not determined by force. If force were to be used, everything would be over immediately. If the communists had had their way, everything would be over. The fallen world, which used to show off its mighty armies that created such a history of strife in this earthly world, and which passed down Satan's tradition, will have a miserable end.

God, who knows such things, is trying to bring Satan to surrender naturally. He tells him to do everything He wants. After letting him do everything he wants, Heaven will be hit first and then it will take it all away, saying that the one who struck the side of justice must pay for all the damages. When Satan arrives at the end of the world, he will be left with nowhere to go. God cannot bring this to pass by Himself.

Rather, He has to prepare a person on earth who can inherit this task. This is why He sends the Messiah in the Last Days.[5]

---

5 Cheon Seong Gyeong: (210-231, 1990.12.23)

Sun Myung Moon as a strikingly practical messiah saw that the Kingdom would require new institutions and organizations as all the old, under the dominion of Satan and his minions, were corrupt. So, the United Nations, media, the academic realm, industries and the arts would have to recreated. Such could not be done by fiat or magic but by "reborn" individuals and families.

If there was anything he was famous for it was his mass weddings which clashed profoundly with the traditional concepts of romantic bliss. But Sun Myung Moon saw families centered on God as the realistic foundation for the Kingdom of God on Earth[6], the fulfillment both of the original three blessings in the Garden of Eden and Jesus' counsel to Nicodemus: "You must be born again" (John 3:1-21). In fact, he saw giving the "Blessing" to millions of couples as the essence of Jesus' mission which he sought to fulfill.[7]

Sun Myung Moon's earthly death or "ascension", as his followers call the beginning of the third stage of life, took place Sept. 3, 2012, without that goal of establishing the "Kingdom" being achieved.

---

6 Once the Blessing of 360,000 couples gives way to the Blessing of 3.6 million, 36 million, 360 million and finally 3.6 billion couples, human society will finally see the eradication of AIDS and the realization of a world of pure true love, where God and humankind are united into one. This is not a mere dream. God's great work of establishing the Kingdom of Heaven on earth, the realization of this providence, is an inevitable truth. That is because it is the not the work of one human being, but the work of God. (271-99, 1995.8.23)

7 Forty years ago, in order to explain the Second Advent of the Lord, I had to go through the sixty-six books of the Bible, but now there is no need to even talk about the Second Advent. When asked, "Do you know Rev. Moon?" the answer would be that he is the man who has blessed 360,000 couples, and will bless 3.6 million couples in the not too distant future. One might ask, "Is he an ordinary person or the Messiah?" Considering all he has done, the right answer would be that he is the Messiah; no one would think that he was just an ordinary person. (275-66, 1995.11.3)

'Three generation kingship'

The Second Coming was over.

With the tragic divisions in his family, it seemed to some that the world had returned with a vengeance to its status of Kingdom of Hell with all the evils that entailed. His wife, Hak Ja Han who had seemingly prevailed in an exceedingly difficult mission, proclaimed herself the "only begotten daughter of God" and revised the sacrosanct Cheon Seong Gyeong collections of his words about which he had repeatedly directed that not a single change should ever be made. Tellingly, she almost never mentioned his name again.

Enter his youngest son, Hyung Jin "Sean" who "broke his silence" in early 2015 (as Donald J. Trump was emerging as an international political phenomenon) with weekly YouTube sermons from Newfoundland, Pennsylvania. His "remnant" of believers that came to be known as the "Sanctuary Church" were reminded that on three public occasions, two in the United States and one in Korea, he had been anointed and crowned the "heir and successor" by his father, Sun Myung Moon in early 2009.

The significance of this event was the "Three Generation Kingship" which sustained and multiplied the bloodline of Christ on earth: Hyung Jin as the "Second King of Cheun Il Guk" and his third son as the "Third King".

Members of the Sanctuary remnant and others recalled videotaped scenes of a genuinely happy Sun Myung Moon spent playing with and providing early education to the very young "Third King" Shin Joon.

All the above raises questions about the role of the mass

communications media in the 20th and 21st centuries. There were no known media at the time of Jesus and therefore reliable written records of his words and brief ministry were scarce.

Such was not the case with the ministry of Sun Myung Moon. Photographers were usually present at his thousands of public appearances and all of his speeches were recorded. But secular mass media accounts about him were largely negative, focusing on controversies generated by those who attacked him rather than his core teachings.

As earlier noted, a Seoul-based British journalist who also worked for U.S. news organizations, Michael Breen, undertook the laborious task of interviewing all available primary sources about Sun Myung Moon. The result was a fascinating unauthorized biography, "Sun Myung Moon, The Early Years 1920-53" [8] which chronicled both the extreme hardship of life in Japan-occupied Korea and the remarkable spirit-filled underground Christian movements in the 1940s led by charismatics some of whom believed they were to prepare for the returning Christ who would be born in Korea.

Two very rare news articles about Sun Myung Moon that took into account the essence of the man according to him and not just his critics were written by Breen for the Korea Times.

A former correspondent for the Free Press International News Service, The Washington Times and the Guardian, Breen had served more than once as president of the Seoul

---

8   Breen, Michael (1997). Sun Myung Moon: the early years 1920–53. Hurstpierpoint West Sussex, U.K.: Refuge Books. ISBN 978-0953163700.

Foreign Correspondence Club before establishing a success-ful communications consultancy in South Korea. In one article, "Sun Myung Moon, son of a broken-hearted God," Breen noted:[9]

> His ideas depart from the Protestantism of his youth in three significant ways: first, his interpretation of the biblical "fall of man" is that mankind disobeyed God not by eating fruit, but through premature sexual rela-tions; second Jesus Christ did not "come to die," as Christians believe, but that he was murdered before he could marry and have a sinless family as the foundation for a sinless world; and third, that Christ will not return in person, as Christians believe, but that another man and his family will complete the messianic business.

In the second article, an obituary, "Polite Society and Sun Myung Moon", Breen called attention to the role of the mass media in notifying the world of the coming of Sun Myung Moon:[10]

> It's hard to feel sorry for a billionaire, harder if he's regarded by thousands around the world as the messiah.
>
> But spare a thought for Rev. Moon Sun-Myung who in public, outside of his adoring inner circle, never had a single good review. He was vilified and ridiculed most of his adult life. The criticism and hounding of his fol-

9 Polite society and Sun Myung Moon, https://www.cosmictribune.com/polite-society-and-sun-myung-moon/, September 12, 2012
10 Sun Myung Moon: Son of the broken-hearted God, https://www.cosmictribune.com/rev-moon-famous-and-uniquely-korean-is-ill/, August 16, 2012

lowers contemptuously known as "Moonies" have been unrelenting. Why? Not because his beliefs and claims are any more ridiculous than other religious notions, but because they were new.

Everyone, it seemed, had a reason to dislike him. The political left hated him for saying communism was the anti-Christ; Christians said he was anti-Christ; to most, he was a conman who used religion to get rich, a brain-washer of young people, a nut-case who claimed to chat with the dead, a man who broke up families, who had a factory that made weapons, who wanted to control the White House, and maybe take over the world.

Satisfied with this media interpretation, society failed to ask the right questions about what Moon stood for and whether he was really that dangerous. As a result, even democracies put him on the blacklist with known terrorists. He was banned for decades from Japan and most European countries.

If his story presents an unflattering example of how most societies are incapable of handling heretics in a dignified and democratic manner, it is also a modern example of the ancient phenomenon of how religion is born.

For Moon's real offense is to be a modern-day Jesus, to have something new to say about God and to assume that doing so makes him spiritually superior to the rest of us.

So as is true of the enormous impact Jesus of Nazareth made on Earth, the mission of Sun Myung Moon and his direct lineal descendants is an unfolding story. But it has put the concept of "Christ on Earth" back on the table.

Should strictly secular mass media cover such matters of faith that are central to the private lives of most? And if so, how?

Yes. With both objectivity and respect.

In conclusion, was Jesus of Nazareth who he said he was?[11] And did Christ return during the apocalyptic century just concluded?

Were the news media justified in dismissing Sun Myung Moon as illegitimate and unworthy of coverage?

Or, to the contrary, will the true historical record conclude that the fourth estate missed "the Second Coming," the greatest story of all time?

---

11 Mark 14: 60-62: 60 Then the high priest stood up before them and asked Jesus, "Are you not going to answer? What is this testimony that these men are bringing against you?" 61 But Jesus remained silent and gave no answer.

Again the high priest asked him, "Are you the Messiah, the Son of the Blessed One?"

62 "I am," said Jesus. "And you will see the Son of Man sitting at the right hand of the Mighty One and coming on the clouds of heaven."

WHAT I SAW AT THE SECOND COMING...

POSTSCRIPT

Finally, a word about "journalistic objectivity".

Journalists in the pre-Trump era insisted that they had no opinions and merely reported the facts. All opinions, political persuasions and religious or ideological beliefs were checked at the door before we sat down at the keyboard.

Really?

Secular humanist and politically correct views dominate the consensus to which most 21st century news professionals adhere in order to establish their credibility, a prerequisite for being taken seriously, i.e., keeping their jobs.

So, can a journalist who was a "participant-observer" in the media founded by Sun Myung Moon be a credible witness?

"Participant-observer" was the term suggested by my thesis committee on the faculty of the University of Texas Journalism Department for characterizing my role in writing "The Making of a New Metropolitan Daily in New York: The News World."[1] I was after all an "insider" with a unique understanding of the genesis of Sun Myung Moon's first American newspaper. But as a journalist charged with writing a scholarly work that compared this newspaper with the New York Times and the Christian Science Monitor [all three newspapers having ties with organized religion], I was required to take a step back from that of an advocate of the new religion and its media.

---

1   Republished in the book, "The News World of New York City: A Retrospective", Origin 2021 Publishing, 2023.

Interestingly, Sun Myung Moon took the same approach in witnessing to new followers of his rapidly expanding evangelistic movement throughout the last half of the 20th century. Likewise, introductory seminars about his "Divine Principle" made no claims about his identity as the "Lord of the Second Advent" but did credit him as the author of the "Divine Principle" and its outline and explanation of Biblical history from Adam and Eve to Jesus and up to the present.

Readers' "faith" may influence what they decide to believe when reading social media and conventional media accounts.

The author's "faith" is his own business. But he has upheld high standards of "journalistic objectivity" reinforced by Judeo Christian values throughout his career while at the same time tracking and studying Sun Myung Moon's teachings, his directives and his media operations.

So, this has been a "participant-observer" account written from the perspective of Sun Myung Moon's faith community.

What was the Founder's motive for spending billions of dollars from his businesses on secular media that did not, unlike the Christian Science Monitor, publish his teachings except as paid advertisements? Was it PR or a direct challenge to the powerful arbiters of reason and reality that are aligned with Godless ideologies?

Readers can and should check the record, connect the dots, and reach their own conclusions.